ADVANCE PRAISE

"*That it May be Well With You* is a splendid book. It is more than a history of the founding of the House of Ruth Maryland; the book provides a detailed and fascinating account of how a small group of passionate community organizers created a critically needed refuge for victims of interpersonal violence."

  – Richard J. Gelles, Ph.D.

   Dean

   School of Social Policy & Practice

   University of Pennsylvania

That It May Be Well With You

The Founding of
House of Ruth Maryland

Kathleen O'Ferrall Friedman and Barbara J. Parker

Then Naomi, her mother in law, said to her,
My daughter, shall I not seek rest for you, that it
may be well with you?

– *"Book of Ruth," American King James Bible*

That It May Be Well With You

The Founding of
House of Ruth Maryland

Kathleen O'Ferrall Friedman and Barbara J. Parker

Apprentice House
Baltimore, Maryland

First Edition

Printed in the United States of America

Paperback ISBN: 978-1-62720-024-0
Ebook ISBN: 978-1-62720-025-7

Design by Cymone Gosnell

Published by Apprentice House

Apprentice House
Loyola University Maryland
4501 N. Charles Street
Baltimore, MD 21210
410.617.5265 • 410.617.2198 (fax)
www.ApprenticeHouse.com
info@ApprenticeHouse.com

Contents

DEDICATION

We dedicate this book to our husbands
Richard W. Friedman and Dale N. Schumacher.
Their support as we did this work in the 1970s and
continuing with writing this book has been invaluable.

PREFACE

In the spring of 2013, House of Ruth Maryland Executive Director Sandi Timmons summarized the 35-year growth of one of the nation's leading intimate partner violence centers: "What began as a row house haven for battered women, has grown to an agency that last year served over 9,000 victims through our comprehensive services that include legal, counseling, shelter and rapid re-housing programs—plus thousands more through trainings, community outreach and our abuse intervention program."

When the seeds were sown for The House of Ruth in the 1970s, the issue of intimate partner abuse was not well understood or documented. There were few places of refuge for abused women and their children. In fact, throughout history, societies around the globe had sanctioned, tolerated or ignored violence against women. Far too many continue that pattern today.

This story of how a small group of earnest, determined women came together in Baltimore to combat such violence provides not only an historical account of the development of a vital program, but also an inspiring blueprint for practical, results-oriented social activism in today's society.

This history was written by two of the "founding mothers" of the House of Ruth. As sources we have relied on our own memories, boxes of articles and documents carefully kept by Kathleen O'Ferrall Friedman, records at the House of Ruth found by helpful staff, archives at the Enoch Pratt Library, the Greater Homewood Association, Maryland Historical Society and University of Baltimore. Additionally, we sent a questionnaire and interviewed many friends and colleagues. Comments from the questionnaires are noted as the individual's questionnaire in the text. We have undertaken this task to document our history and to hopefully inspire others to take on social issues even if the immediate answers are unknown.

In the oft-quoted words of Margaret Mead:

> *"Never doubt that a small group of thoughtful, committed citizens can change the world. Indeed, it is the only thing that ever has."*

INTRODUCTION

The journey of many women is reflected in the personal story of Brenda Finch:

For five years, I was subjected to beatings, torture and putdowns by my husband. After a great deal of reflection, I began to object. I was changing inside and no longer felt I deserved those beatings. I realized I had to just walk away without looking back. It wasn't easy. In October 1977, I slept in doorways when there was no other place to go. But then I read about a new shelter opening in Baltimore and, soon after, I telephoned the House of Ruth. In November, I entered the shelter as its second resident and found refuge there. I left the House of Ruth in March 1978, having found in it the friendly arm I hadn't before... (Let Her Voice Be Heard)

Finch later became a peer counselor and helped other women to recover from abuse and to begin new lives. She was an integral part of the early days of the House of Ruth, a program borne out of years of research, planning and advocacy in the 1970s.

The movement to establish a shelter in Baltimore began with an awakening, both on a national and local scale, not only to the economic and political circumstances of women, but also to the serious problem of spousal abuse and the need for protection of women from abuse by their husbands. As awareness increased about the extent of the social problem, the movement expanded to include protection for any woman abused by a man in her life, married or single.

> *One battered wife who brought herself to the*
> *point of sharing her secret with a friend was*
> *surprised when the friend responded, "So what's a*
> *little slapping around?"*
> – *Marcella Schuyler*

Over the years, the terminology to categorize the violence changed. At first, the prevalent term was "battered wife syndrome," adapted from the concept of the "battered child syndrome" that had been identified by medical researchers and service providers in the early 1960s. After social scientists began to investigate and write about abused women, finding the word "syndrome" inapplicable, the term "battered women" took hold. (Under current Maryland law there is a defense to murder and aggravated assault called the "Battered Spouse or Battered Woman's Syndrome," MD Code, Cts. & Jud. Pro. § 10-916.) The broader term "domestic violence" began to be used to encompass spouses and domestic partners irrespective of gender. As decades

have passed, "intimate partner violence" has become the
operative phrase, reflecting a broader understanding of the
social problem and inclusiveness of those involved. Still,
statistically, violence against women by intimate partners
is greater by far than violence against men by intimate
partners.

The awakening was occurring for women in the social
work, health and nursing professions who saw other women
with unexplained or unlikely causes of injuries receiving
treatment for their injuries, but without interventions
that would keep them safe in the future. The more their
eyes opened to the likelihood of spousal abuse, the more
frequently they asked themselves, "What can I do to change
this pattern? What can I do to make the system work better
for these women?" They saw the need to act and shed light
on the immense social ill of battered women. Through
efforts to educate the public about the problems facing
battered women, women professionals, social organizations
and women from all walks of life began to network, looking
for solutions to prevent abuse of women and to intervene
and treat it appropriately when it occurred.

At first, these women framed the issue intuitively—
gathering data about incidences of abuse; identifying the
responses to women seeking help from hospitals, social
agencies, police, courts and lawyers; collecting what little
statistics were available; and reaching out to the media to
raise public awareness. These women gradually coalesced
into a critical mass through women's organizations, some

established and some newly created. With passion and determination, they took action to effect legislative changes, to reform the criminal justice system, and to establish a crisis shelter.

Simultaneously, throughout the country in cities such as Ann Arbor, Boston, Los Angeles, Miami, Minneapolis-St. Paul, New York City, and Washington, D.C., and across the Atlantic Ocean in London, similar efforts were unfolding.

In June 1977, The House of Ruth, Baltimore, Inc., now known as House of Ruth Maryland, formed as a charitable and educational corporation to provide shelter and counseling for battered women. In November of that year, the crisis shelter opened in a Calvert Street row house in downtown Baltimore. In less than a decade, the issue of intimate partner violence moved from a hidden social ill to public acknowledgement. Battered women shelters were established around the country.

To set the stage for this historical narrative, one must look back to the 1960s, a period of upheaval and great social change in America. The rules of societal engagement were rigid and exclusionary for blacks, the elderly, women and others who did not fit into what were considered traditional roles. Within the family, men and women had ascribed gender roles—men superior and women inferior (O'Brien, 1971) Despite increases in women college students in the 1920s to 1950s, and women's involvement in the war effort during World War II, post-war American women experienced a lower social, economic and political status than men. Women, for the most part, lived narrow lives relegated to the home, motherhood and associated activities. It is disquieting to recall the inequities that existed in daily life. Family violence was a secret.

Women's Rights in the 1960s

A young woman today would be disconcerted to learn that, if she was coming of age 50 years ago, she could be denied much of what is currently taken for granted. In spite of having the right to vote, if she did not take her husband's name as expected upon marriage, she would be prohibited from voting under her own name. Moreover, she could obtain credit only in her husband's name. Women generally were prevented from entering professions—except teaching, social work and nursing—and were virtually barred from corporate management. Those who worked outside the home in clerical positions, factory work, retail sales and service jobs did not receive equal pay for equal work (a situation that has only improved slightly today) Most private colleges and universities were open only to men. In the 1960s, women had to have permission from their husbands to have a tubal ligation, a permanent method of birth control.

To understand what compelled women to deal with societal problems such as violence against women, it is necessary to appreciate the will and drive that developed in women in all spheres of society. Many women were inspired by the civil rights movement to seek fuller lives and equality of rights under the law. However, some women involved in the civil rights movement reported that they were treated like clerical help or asked to make the coffee during many civil rights endeavors. (Hayden & King, 1966)

Political Acknowledgement

In 1961, responding to a growing national interest in women's rights, President John F. Kennedy appointed a commission, the President's Commission on the Status of Women (PCSW), chaired by former First Lady Eleanor Roosevelt. In Executive Order 10980 that established the PCSW, President Kennedy recognized at that time "prejudices and outmoded customs act as barriers to the full realization of women's basic rights ..." (Lewis, undated)

At the same time, Congress dealt with numerous initiatives regarding the status of women, which resulted in the passage of the 1963 Equal Pay Act requiring equal pay for men and women doing equal work. The following year, Congress passed Title VII of the Civil Rights Act, prohibiting employers from discriminating against women in employment. Unfortunately, these laws did not result in noticeable change for the wages and types of jobs of women. (Lewis) The 1965 PCSW report, which noted the discriminatory wages of women and the declining ratio of women in professional and executive jobs and made specific recommendations, "was duly buried in bureaucratic file drawers." (Friedan, 1963) Betty Friedan's eye-opening *The Feminine Mystique*, published in 1963, along with women's

frustration over the lack of any meaningful change, led
Friedan and others to form the National Organization for
Women (NOW) Feeling empowered, women decided to
take matters into their own hands and create their own
movement, known as The Women's Liberation Movement.

Workforce Considerations

By the 1970s, the most significant development in the
economy was the influx of women into the work force,
rising to more than 43 percent, up from 29 percent in the
1950s. Employment opportunities remained narrow in lower
paying jobs—clerical, sales, and service jobs. Forty percent
of employed women were concentrated in clerical work. By
1975, nearly two-fifths of all workers were women, although
concentrated in less skilled occupations, receiving less pay
than men for similar work. (Waite, 1981)

ERA

In 1972, Congress passed the Equal Rights Amendment
(ERA), first proposed by suffragist and women's rights
activist Alice Paul in 1923, and sent it to the states for
ratification by the congressionally imposed deadline of
June 30, 1982. Only 35 of the three-fourths of the states
required by the constitution (38 of 50) ratified the ERA
by the deadline. (Napikoski, no date) With lobbying by the
Maryland Chapter of NOW and women legislators pressing
for ratification, Maryland was one of the states to ratify
the ERA. In November 1972, Maryland voters accepted
the Maryland Equal Rights Amendment by a two to one

margin. Effective January 1, 1973, it was the expected
impetus to important change in the status of women under
the law in Maryland.

(Report to Governor, Governor's Commission to Study
Implementation of the Equal Rights Amendment)

Inspired by the burgeoning feminist movement, passage
of the Maryland Equal Rights Amendment, enactment of
protective laws for women, and their own vision for the
future, women began to observe the inequality in their
business, professional and social lives and in the lives of
those around them. As much as they perceived society's
discrimination against themselves, they realized that women
experienced greater hardships including brutality by their
husbands.

II. Awareness Spurs Action in Baltimore

As women began to graduate from law schools, the Legal Aid Bureau (LAB) began to hire them in its Baltimore office. It was one of the few law firms to hire women in the early 1970s. The Bureau then, as it does now, provided legal assistance to the poor, with an overriding commitment to social justice. Young attorneys dedicated themselves to public interest law in the hopes of changing the world. Representing Legal Aid clients brought to these young lawyers a deeper awareness of existing social problems, including battered women.

Divorce Cases; Hidden Violence

LAB lawyers were "consistently amazed at the number of women" who sought divorces for vague reasons but finally admitted they had been beaten repeatedly. (Worobec, 1977) An alarming number of women were living in home situations fraught with violence. They were young, middle-aged and older women. They were tired, desperate, and in need of assistance to get away from the intimidation and brutality. Most had never told anyone. Those who had sought support from other family members had been told to go home and be better wives.

Collaborating with other lawyers at the Bureau on individually assigned cases, LAB lawyers discovered that a significant number of women clients seeking divorces revealed a whole range of violence against them by their husbands. Many had not left their husbands because of the lack of funds and no other place to live.

From the high number of battered women seeking legal advice, LAB lawyers realized that intervening on a case-by-case basis through criminal charges and complaints for divorce, although necessary for the wife's protection from physical injury, did not address prevention. Furthermore, divorce cases did not raise issues that could be addressed through litigation seeking reform. The larger picture demanded study of the problem to find creative ways to effect change in the criminal and domestic law, to more effectively represent clients complaining of abuse, and moreover, to bring about social change. It required a special project with these broader goals.

Beyond the Criminal Justice System

LAB lawyers thought medical and social agencies needed to address the problem as well. The need to engage other professional women — social workers, nurses, educators, businesswomen and volunteers — in the movement to protect battered wives became increasingly apparent. Officials in the criminal justice system were not applying existing criminal law in assault cases involving wife abuse and civil remedies were not available, requiring legislative reform. It was going to take legislation enacted by the General Assembly to provide adequate protection from violence for women. Successful legislation needed public support and a lobbying effort by representatives from all the disciplines in contact with these women seeking help. Solutions for this social problem required more comprehensive intervention strategies.

III. Battered Women Project

With the support of Joseph A. Matera, Executive Director of the LAB (and continuing with his successor Charles H. Dorsey), Kathleen (Katy) O'Ferrall Friedman, Carolyn Rodis and Hazel Warnick, staff attorneys in the Domestic Law Unit of the Baltimore LAB, created the Battered Women Project in 1972. They chose the term "battered women" instead of "battered wives" to widen the protective umbrella. The operative definition of a battered woman within the movement that evolved to combat such violence was "one who receives deliberate and repeated physical injury from a man with whom she has a primary relationship (married, separated, lover [now referred to as intimate partner])." (Battered Women: A Handbook)

> *In the course of representing women in domestic cases, I was exposed for the first time to issues of battering, both women and children. Although I suppose I knew such things existed, it was eye-opening to hear these women's stories and to discover how prevalent domestic battering*

*actually was. It was also eye opening and
frustrating to realize how few legal protections
existed at the time.*
    – Hazel Warnick

The Battered Women Project attempted to examine
the problem areas and to recommend legal intervention.
As a first step, LAB attorneys identified the high incidence
of wife beating in their domestic caseloads and developed
standards for handling their individual cases during
appearances before the courts. Carolyn Rodis recounted
that "a third of her caseload was women escaping abusive
marriages and relationships." "We had to educate the
judges … about the dangers faced by these women," she
commented. (Rodis Questionnaire)

*I remember one client who was in her 80s. She
had been abused for years, and finally had had
enough. She had courage to leave him and create
a new life for herself. Another client was very
young, maybe a teenager, when I represented her.
Several years later, after I had left Legal Aid, I
ran into her at a Giant Food store, where she was
a cashier. She was making good money, she was
confident and competent, told me about her child,
and seemed happy in her life.*
    – Carolyn Rodis

I remember several cases where I was able to open the eyes of Judge Watts (Judge Robert B. Watts, Circuit Court for Baltimore City) to the dangers facing my clients. In one case, he allowed the woman to remain in his chambers rather than in the courtroom until her case was called, so she didn't have to interact with, and feel threatened by, her husband. In another case, I think he allowed the women to remain in his chambers until the man was escorted out of the courthouse –or he had the man stay behind until she was safely away. We realized that being safe for that hour wasn't enough for the woman; she needed a safe place to go. (Rodis Questionnaire)

University of Maryland School of Social Work

With heavy caseloads, the lawyers could not take time away from working with clients, case preparation and court appearances to address organizing for social change. Community organizing was neither within their skill set nor a part of their job specifications. Recognizing this, Katy Friedman contacted the University of Maryland School of Social Work and Community Planning (UMSSWCP) and talked with the director of social strategy field placements (which encompassed community organization) The director agreed to assign School of Social Work students to the LAB.

The Legal Aid Bureau needed the aid of someone with community organizing skills. Richard

Friedman, a social worker and my husband,
suggested that I contact the University of
Maryland School of Social Work and Community
Planning to request a student field placement
assignment with the Bureau. He thought they
would agree to such a proposal because I have
both a law degree and a master's degree in social
work.

   – Katy O'Ferrall Friedman

Over a period of three years (1973–1975), the School
of Social Work assigned three students in their final year of
studies to the Battered Women Project, one each fall. The
students were being trained as community organizers in a
curriculum geared to teach them to create social change.
Friedman, who had a master's degree in social work,
functioned as task supervisor while a social work professor
acted as field supervisor. The first two students assigned
to the project concentrated on assessing the problem and
investigating the response of the criminal justice system.

   Kathleen (Kee) Hall, who had a fine arts degree, came
to the LAB in October 1973. In her social work studies,
she had learned about the battered child syndrome, which
inspired a deep commitment to family violence intervention
and a desire to raise public consciousness about violence
against women. Her task was to analyze the battered
spouse problem and define it from a societal point of view.
Hall interviewed LAB lawyers and clients, observed court

hearings, and met with police and court commissioners. Journalist Enid Sefcovic wrote about Hall's findings in a June 18, 1975 article, "Battered Wives: A Shelter from The Pain" published by the now-defunct *Baltimore News American*. Quoting extensively from Hall, Friedman and Kathleen McDonald, chair of the Maryland Commission on the Status of Women (MCSW) task force to establish a shelter, the article reported the inadequate response from the criminal justice system, the existing bias against women permeating all levels of society, and the need for a crisis shelter.

Sheila Bittner, the second student assigned to a field placement at the LAB project in fall 1974, was newly married and somewhat reserved. She began to gather the smattering of relevant articles that appeared in national magazines and newspapers at the time. Her collection resulted in the information needed to describe the social problem from a national perspective and beyond.

Marcella Schuyler, the third and last student to be placed at the LAB by the School of Social Work for the Battered Women Project, arrived in September 1975. Schuyler brought tremendous energy, insight and skill to the effort. Ultimately, she became the first president of The House of Ruth, Baltimore, Inc.

> *While a 19-year-old undergraduate, Marcella*
> *worked as a summer intern with my husband*
> *Richard Friedman at the Maryland Children's*

Center in Arbutus. I connected with her when she was working in a field placement at the Maryland Conference of Social Concern with Alice Williams who graduated from UMSSWCP the same year as Richard. This is "Smalltimore."
– *Katy O'Ferrall Friedman*

Motivated by the community organizing skills of writer and activist Saul Alinsky, who preached that power came from the bottom up, Schuyler tackled the project with panache. Using community organization principles identified by George Brager and Harry Sprecht in their book *Community Organizing*, she developed a proposal as a part of her academic requirements. "An Analysis of the Battered Wives Problem," gave form and process to the LAB project. It became the blueprint for the movement toward the goal of a crisis shelter to house battered women.

Schuyler's analysis showed that social change involves two phases. First, it is necessary to frame the issues of the problem to arouse public awareness and then, using the framework, mobilize participants to action. (Schuyler, "An Analysis of the Battered Women Problem," p.1) What the LAB lawyers had been doing intuitively became an educated and systematic process. They were on the right track and, moreover, now they had the person, as she herself put it, "with fire in her belly" to make it happen. (Schuyler interview, March 2013)

IV. Framing the Issues

The LAB attorneys and social work students spent
1973 through 1976 educating themselves about the history
of the social roles of women and men, investigating the
current official response to the abuse of women when they
sought assistance from the criminal justice system, reviewing
available academic literature and gathering statistics on
intimate violence. Whenever they could, they took this
information to the public and to professional entities to
make the case. They worked to effect change in police,
prosecutors', court commissioners' and judges' policies and
practices.

Challenges to Justice

Hall's investigation of the criminal justice system
resulted in identifying a pattern of treatment by police,
court commissioners and courts that indicated a failed
system unable or unwilling to provide adequate protection
for women. She reported that when women tried to leave
abusive relationships, their husbands often hounded and
sometimes stalked them. Without money, with children

to support and fearful of facing the world alone, they often returned home because the obstacles seemed insurmountable. Police responding to calls about battering offered no assistance or intervention. Hall remarked, "[The women] are intimidated by the police who dismiss repeated incidents as family quarrels, or who accept a husband's phony (sic) story and ignore bruises." (Sefcovic, 1975)

Clients reported to LAB lawyers and to Hall that police did not arrest the offenders, and offered the victims little advice about how to file a complaint. Police insisted that, for them to intervene, a woman would have to obtain a legal separation, which did not exist in Maryland. A spokesman for the Baltimore City Police Department identified a shortcoming in the law. "Usually, the woman wants the man thrown out, which we can't do if they're both residents there. She's required to swear out a warrant." (Sefcovic, 1975) Yet, some police officers were not complying with their duty to file a complaint report at the district police station, nor were they telling the abused women that they could go to the district station and request an arrest warrant or a summons from a court commissioner.

When the abused women found their way to the court commissioner's office, they were again met with indifference. A court commissioner is an appointed employee (usually a non-lawyer) designated to determine probable cause to issue a warrant or summons based on the complainant's allegations and/or the police report. Hall observed that "they are frustrated by court commissioners who will not give them warrants and, instead, say: 'Get a divorce.'" Court commissioners, based on their personal frustration, hesitated to provide assistance by granting warrants or summonses because some women made repeated requests and because women often did not show up in court. Hall quoted a court commissioner who stated, "In order to solve the battered wife problem, you'd have to bomb East Baltimore." (Sefcovic, 1975)

The few cases that reached the court met weak responses from judges who were lenient with male abusers. The judges also expressed frustration with women who dropped charges or reconciled with their husbands. The judges were resistant toward these types of cases, believing them to be domestic matters which should be handled in civil court. They empathized with working men and fathers of children. Even in a case where a husband shot his wife, who nearly died, the husband was not sent to jail because his employer testified that he was a good worker. (Battered Women: A Handbook, 1978)

The information gleaned by Hall provided talking points when the volunteers approached the community to gather support for the cause and the criminal justice system to urge proper and effective handling of the problem. Relying on these observations of system failures, LAB negotiated improved handling of victims of inter-spousal violence with the police, courts and State's Attorney's Office. The then-administrative judge of the District Court of Maryland, Baltimore City, responded favorably with permission to allow training of court commissioners and full support of judicial training. However, training of commissioners did not take place until 1978 and, for judges, even later.

Working with clients first hand, LAB staff attorneys quickly realized the scope of the problem. Hazel Warnick, raised in a family not exposed to violence, was taken aback at representing many battered women in court. "Sharing stories with other lawyers at the Bureau," observed Warnick, "made it clear that this was a large problem that desperately needed to be addressed." The lack of sufficient laws and safe places of refuge for her clients and their children frustrated Warnick. (Warnick Questionnaire) Both she and Carolyn Rodis found the law lacking any method of protecting battered women. As much as they felt laws were inadequate to protect women, they also thought the medical and social systems needed to provide treatment for these violent offenders. (Worobec, 1977)

A Model Program in London

Bittner discovered a newspaper article that referred to Erin Pizzey, founder of Women's Aid, a national center for battered women begun in 1970 in Chiswick, London, England. Pizzey had grown up in a home where her alcoholic father routinely beat her mother. As an adult, she dedicated herself to educating the British public about battered women and creating shelters with the aid of a construction business owner and a Labour party member of Parliament committed to helping underprivileged people.

Her first refuge opened in 1971. (Ashby & Pizzey, 1974, p. 6)

Bittner contacted Pizzey to gather information and learned about the bold strategy of her grassroots movement in London. The connection with Pizzey and the relationship that developed between her and those involved in the movement in this country provided momentum for shelters for battered women. Pizzey played a vital role in the founding of the House of Ruth.

National Media

The first national magazine to publish an article about battered women was *Ladies Home Journal.* Karin Durban's article entitled "Wife-Beating" appeared in the June 1974 issue. The exposé about middle-class women beaten by their husbands bemoaned the lack of reliable statistics about the incidence of wife abuse. The article reported, "Legal experts think that wife abuse is one of the most underreported crimes in the country—even more underreported than rape, which the FBI estimates is 10 times more frequent than statistics indicate. A conservative estimate puts the number of battered wives nationwide at well over a million." (Durban, 1974, p. 64) The main thrust of the article was an insightful examination of the economic and psychological reasons that battered women felt compelled to stay with their husbands. Surprisingly, *Ms.* magazine, noted for its progressive views on women's equality, did not publish an article about spousal abuse until August 1976. (Gingold, 1976)

In October 1975, the *New York Times* published a
two-part article on battered women, one of them by Del
Martin, a former NOW national board member, who was
writing a book on battered wives that was published a year
later. Martin referenced Pizzey, whose book *Scream Quietly
or the Neighbors Will Hear*, published in England in 1974,
became an important resource in the battered women
movement. In 1977, her book was published in America.
(Pizzey, 1977)

Historical Basis; Laws and Attitudes

Schuyler, following the Brager and Sprecht concept of
framing the issue, gathered information about the social
roles of men and women, the inadequate response of the
criminal justice system to the problem, and statistical data
about the incidence of battering. She found that there was a
"tacit assumption that a man's wife is his property to do with
as he pleases." (Schuyler, 1975) Schuyler reported, "This
assumption, which can be traced historically from Biblical
quotations, has been re-enforced by legal statute spanning
from the Napoleonic Code where it was stated 'women, like
walnut trees, should be beaten every day' to present laws."
(Schuyler, 1975)

Laws in colonial America were rooted in English
common law, including the marriage contract. Marriage
suspended the woman's legal existence which was
incorporated into that of the husband. Under English
common law, wife beating was permitted. *Blackstone's*

Commentaries allowed that a husband had the power to restrain his wife with degrees of physical punishment depending upon the degrees of her misdeeds. (Blackstone) In Colonial America, Puritans discouraged family violence, but in other areas of the New World "men were expected to exercise moderate 'chastisement' from time to time." (Plummer, quoting Fischer, 2006, p. 1)

By the 1890s, most states prohibited a man from beating his wife. In Maryland, ironically, the penalty for wife abuse prescribed by statute was a whipping "not to exceed 40 lashes." Del Martin posited in *Battered Wives,* published in 1976, that the patriarchal marriage contract fostered wife abuse because it suspended her legal existence and made her a legal dependent. The failure of meaningful intervention by the criminal justice system, Schuyler insisted, "... reinforced the notion that it is a husband's right to beat his wife." (Schuyler, 1975)

Another issue was that hitting or slapping women was generally considered funny or the source of jokes. Jackie Gleason, a famous comedian, was known for saying to his fictional TV wife: "One of these days, Alice ... BAM! Right in the kisser!" while brandishing his fists. This always received a large laugh.

As this was early in the women's movement, most abused women were embarrassed about the abuse, believed that they were the only one, and believed it when their husbands said that they deserved it. Unfortunately, many religious organizations and religious leaders counseled women that it was their responsibility to keep the family together by whatever means.

Local Strategy; Telling the Story

Following Schuyler's blueprint and using the models of the London Women's Aid and the Ann Arbor-Washtenaw County NOW Wife Assault Task Force, the LAB Battered Women Project developed a formal strategy to publicize the issue and draw together concerned interest groups and individuals to legitimize it through media and public discussion. The project leaders used the available historical information about the status of women, what little statistical data they had, and growing information from around the country and abroad about battered women, to raise public consciousness. Schuyler emphasized the value of "the story," and espoused the idea that converts can be made by just hearing a good story, what in literary writing is called "narrative."

In an effort to tell the story, they addressed meetings of benevolent associations, service organizations and any congregation of people willing to listen. One of Schuyler's early contacts was a group called Women in Self Help (WISH) Begun in 1974 by professional psychologists and social workers and staffed by volunteers, WISH was the first telephone counseling service for women in the Baltimore area. (Mendeloff Interview) WISH volunteers listened to women with an array of problems, counseled them and referred them to appropriate local, state and private service agencies. (Renhert, 1978)

In 1976, Barbara J. Parker, representing the University of Maryland School of Nursing, and Friedman from the LAB, participated in a panel discussion about battered women at Howard University in Washington, D.C. One of the remarkable presentations at that program addressed violence and societal attitudes toward sexuality. In October of that year, Parker and Friedman attended a national conference of NOW in Philadelphia, which for the first time included wife beating on its agenda. Materials from other efforts, such as the Ann Arbor project, and two pamphlets by Betsy Warrior (1975a, 1975b) were obtained at the conference.

LAB lawyers and representatives from the Baltimore Chapter of NOW appeared on radio and television talk shows to discuss the problem and shed light on relevant questions, including "What causes spousal violence? When beaten, instead of leaving, why do wives stay with their husband? What are the police, court commissioners, courts, hospital personnel and social agencies doing or not doing to intervene? What resources, if any, are available to help battered women?"

To attempt to answer some of these questions, the project leaders relied on the early work of researchers studying violence in the home such as Richard J. Gelles, Murray A. Straus, and Suzanne K. Steinmetz. These social scientists were examining violence in the home at a time when it was largely ignored and unrecognized as a social problem. *Battered Women: A Handbook*, prepared in 1977 and revised in 1978 by the Baltimore Task Force on Battered Women (discussed below), summarized the results of their findings to aid those preparing and making presentations. Together the three social scientists conducted a survey for the National Commission on the Causes and Prevention of Violence; they found that both men (one out of four) and women (one out of six) condoned slapping a wife in certain situations. (*Battered Women: A Handbook* citing Straus, Gelles, and Steinmetz) The national survey found the following:

"… approximately 28% of all American couples have a 'violent episode' at some time during their marriage. By 'violent episode' the researches mean any act causing physical pain or injury from slapping to beating. Of the population surveyed 1 out of 6 had a violent episode during the survey year. About 1 out of every 100 couples had gone … to actually beating their spouse . … Almost 4% had gone so far as to have actually used a knife or gun in their attack. This means that of the 41 million couples living together in the United States almost 1.7 million have at some time faced a knife or gun in an attack by their partner. (*Battered Women: A Handbook*, citing *The New York Times*, December 8, 1976, p.2)

A separate study conducted by Gelles, examining the reason abused wives stay with their husbands, found that the person abused, no matter how grave the bruising, often minimized the incident. (*Battered Women: A Handbook* citing Gelles) Gelles noted that the frequency and severity of the violence, risk to children, and access to financial and other resources increased the likelihood that an abused wife would leave the marriage. (Gelles, 1976)

Educating the public, not only about the extent of spousal abuse but also the official inaction in response to it, became important strategy in combating the social problem. Schuyler emphasized what others in the movement had previously noted, "It was not just the criminal justice agencies that failed to protect women, but also the 'helpers' of society such as medical and social agencies who needed to be convinced to re-frame their thinking." (Schuyler interview)

Media Exposure

Newspaper articles began to appear in 1975. Both the *Sunday Sun* in July 1975 and *The Baltimore Sun* in fall 1975 published columns on battered wives. Newspaper articles by Bill Peterson also appeared in *The Washington Post* in the fall of 1975. One article addressed the frustration of battered wives that resulted from the police, courts and hospitals not keeping records on the wife-beating problem. He affirmed that the problem "rarely gets public attention." (Peterson, 1975)

In order to get the public's attention, Schuyler contacted area and regional newspapers with information and informed sources, hoping to increase their reporting on the subject. WISH volunteers took on the task of conveying the story the public needed to hear to make the problem real. (Schuyler Questionnaire) "Battered Women" became the topic "du jour" as newspapers began to publish articles with increased frequency. On the same day, March 11, 1976, David Lightman's article, "Resolution Would Seek Police Records" appeared in *The Evening Sun* and Gloria Borger's "Abused Wife Demands Help for Sisters" appeared in *The Washington Star*. *The Daily Record*, the local legal and business journal, published "Domestic Violence Sometimes behind Happy Façade of 'Perfect' Marriage," on March 15, 1976. Other articles followed in rapid succession, including:

- March 17, 1976, *The News American* published an article by Enid Sefcovic, "Steps Taken to Help Area Battered Wives."
- March 24, 1976, *The Evening Sun* reported on "Wife Abuse Symposium Scheduled."
- March 29, 1976, Sharon Dickman wrote about "Some Women Put Up with Abuse," *The Evening Sun.*
- March 29, 1976, *The Sun* reported "Beating death laid to husband on probation," by Joseph J. Challmes.
- April 2, 1976, *The News American* carried another column by Enid Sefcovic, "Former Battered Wife Flays Social System."
- July 18, 1976, "Battered wives: Some cope, some quit" by Sharon Dickman appeared in *The Evening Sun.*
- February 4, 1977, *The News American* published

"Expert Feels Violent Behavior Can Be Stopped."
• March 4, 1977, The Daily Record published, "Dear Battered Wife: Take Hint and Leave after First Beating," by Patricia McCormack.

Grassroots Activism

Schuyler generated many ideas to raise public consciousness about battered women. Part of the initiative to educate the public included the Enoch Pratt Library. The Pratt Library in downtown Baltimore has large exhibit windows that face Cathedral Street, which are used to highlight significant library events, foster book reading, and attract public attention to the library. With Friedman's encouragement, Schuyler contacted the Pratt's public relations office to request permission to display material about the problem of battered wives, including Erin Pizzey's *Scream Quietly or the Neighbors Will Hear.* Not only did the library agree to such an exhibit, but insisted that it would put the window display together if the volunteers would provide the material. The window attracted considerable attention for the month it was on display.

> *From the beginning, we believed that if others knew what we were learning about the devastation of battered women, they would immediately join our endeavors and the problem would be solved within a matter of years. So we decided that all we needed to do was inform the public.*
> *– Barbara J. Parker*

During this period, Schuyler and Friedman themselves authored articles on the subject. Schuyler wrote "Battered Wives: An Emerging Social Problem," published in the professional journal *Social Work* in November 1976. By that time, Schuyler was a pupil service worker in Baltimore City Public Schools, and president of the Baltimore Chapter of NOW. Schuyler's article was the first one published on domestic violence in *Social Work*. In her article, Schuyler discussed the emergence of wife abuse as a social problem and proposed strategies for dealing with it. (Schuyler, 1976) Friedman contributed an article to *The University of Maryland Law Forum*, entitled "When Did You Stop Beating Your Wife." This article discussed the inadequate legal relief afforded women subjected to wife-beating and suggested criminal and civil remedies. (Friedman, 1976) A derivative of this article was later published in *It's About NOW*, the Anne Arundel County NOW newsletter. (Friedman, 1978)

Being able to tell the history of societal sanction of abuse against women, describe official inaction to women's complaints, and relate stories of violence against women in a domestic context attracted attention. The success of the public relations campaign using print and electronic media along with public appearances captured the interest of the public on a wide scale. Testifying on legislative proposals concerning inter-spousal abuse before a committee of the General Assembly after the House of Ruth opened in Baltimore, Schuyler remembered, "... It was necessary to

engage in a public relations effort to raise the visibility of
the issue. As needs of battered women became recognized,
a momentum developed making it possible to consider the
establishment of a shelter." (Schuyler, Prepared Testimony,
no date) Statistical data to support assertions of the
widespread incidence of battered women was an additional
element of the case. The volunteer leadership needed to be
able to answer questions about the types of offenses (assault,
aggravated assault, murder), how often women were abused
as opposed to men, and where they went for help.

V. Gathering Statistics

Gathering statistics about the incidence of abuse was a slow process. In 1975, there were still no local or state statistics on the incidence of crimes of violence against women, particularly assault and battery. A 1977 *Women's Rights Law Reporter* article noted: "This lack of statistical evidence on wife assault reflects society's refusal to acknowledge the frequency of family violence." (Eisenberg & Micklow, 1977)   At the time Schuyler wrote her strategic proposal, there was only one attempt to survey the extent of wife abuse in the United States — Ann Arbor-Washtenaw County Wife Assault Task Force, NOW. The data from 1974 police and sheriff files showed an astounding incidence of crimes against wives: assault and battery, felonious assault, intent to murder, and murder. (Fojtik, 1976) Schuyler thought it was a priority "to obtain accurate local statistics about the sex, age and relationship of assault complaints received by the Baltimore City Police Department."

Vital information began to define the issue.

Key Statistics

- A 1974 study of assault victims using the emergency room at Baltimore City Hospital reported 70% of victims were women who had been attacked in their own homes by a husband or lover (Battered Women Handbook, 5)

- In 1975, the Hagerstown Police Department documented that 60% of reported assaults were inter-spousal (between spouses) Women reported 99% of them.

- Federal Bureau of Investigation (FBI), Uniform Crime Reports for the United States published that same year reported an estimated 1.7 million spouses who experienced violence involving a knife or gun.

- More than two million individuals experienced one spouse beating up the other. (Friedman, "The Image of Battered Women" quoting Uniform Crime Reports, Washington, D.C.: Government Printing office, 1974, p. 20)

- On November 3, 1976, *The Daily Record* published a UPI column reporting FBI statistics that, for 1973, a quarter of all murders in the United States occurred within the family and half were husbands killing wives. (Sterling, 1976)

When Parker met Schuyler and Friedman in 1976, they began a long collaboration. Her participation gave the project's efforts to gather local data a considerable boost.

That same year, Parker was finishing a master's degree (MS) and working at Har-Bel, a community health center located on Harford Road in northeast Baltimore. Among the people being seen at the clinic were a large number of women who reported being abused by their husbands.

One of Parker's clients was a tiny short but energetic Catholic woman with six children. Her husband was an alcoholic and they lived with his parents. He was very violent and abusive to her and she received no support from her husband's mother, who had survived a similar experience with her husband. The woman had left her husband several times, but he would come to her place of employment (she was a clerk in a grocery store) and new apartment and make such a ruckus that she was threatened with eviction and the loss of her job. When she sought advice from her priest, she was told that her job was to support her husband in his illness, raise his children, and remember her wedding vows. This woman's helpless, trapped situation—typical of what many women were experiencing in those days—motivated Parker to combine her academic pursuit with an effort to add more information about what she viewed as a major health problem. When Parker reported this woman's abuse to the clinic psychiatrist she was told that the woman must be "secretly enjoying" the abuse, which was a popular Freudian theory of female masochism.

Seeking information beyond the Freudian perspective, Parker looked to social sciences and discovered the work of the Family Violence Research Program, which was established in 1975 at the University of New Hampshire. The work of Murray A. Straus, Richard Gelles and Susan Steinmetz were very influential in developing knowledge on societal and cultural influences in family violence. Gelles published *The Violent Home: A Study of Physical Aggression between Husbands and Wives* in 1972; this publication was extremely helpful to the authors.

Additionally, literature on child abuse by Dr. C. Henry Kempe and associates in the 1960s at the University of Colorado Hospital was instructive. Their work had used social learning theory or the idea that child abusers were often abused themselves as children. This model was helpful in further exploring non-Freudian perspectives on wife abuse.

In reviewing the literature on child abuse, Parker found articles on battered women, primarily from Great Britain. The articles were generally case studies and used terminology such as "granny bashing" and "the wife-beater's wife." She also came across a few newspaper articles in an English newspaper called *The Nursing Times* about Erin Pizzey and her refuges in London.

Friedman was instrumental in helping Parker collect data at the LAB. For this study, all women seeking advice regarding divorce were invited to participate in a survey. A total of 50 women were interviewed; 20 reported current abuse and 30 reported no current abuse. There was no difference between the two groups in terms of age, race, number of children, years of education, years of marriage and the amount of arguing in their nuclear family of origin. Positive findings included: significant relationship between violence in the nuclear family of origin and current abuse; a group of women were seeking divorces following one or two incidences of abuse and did not grow up observing violence, and women who did not observe abuse in their nuclear family were more likely to seek help sooner. (Parker & Schumacher, 1977)

The study did not elaborate on social, cultural, financial, sexual, religious and gender issues that have been investigated in subsequent years. It did, however, promote thinking of the problem beyond Freudian theories in the health field.

Because Parker was using social learning theory based on child abuse research done by others, she titled the phenomena being studied "The Battered Wife Syndrome." Results of the study were published in the *American Journal of Public Health* (AJPH) in August 1977. The study has been identified as the first research study on intimate partner violence published in an established medical journal (Donaldson, 2000) Upon invitation, Friedman submitted an editorial for the same issue. (Friedman, 1977)

In September 1976, the Baltimore Task Force on Battered Women conducted a survey on the experiences and attitudes about abuse from a non-random group of attendees at the Baltimore City Fair. The City Fair was a popular city-sponsored, three-day event with attendance in the tens of thousands. With the cooperation of a local television station, a tent was erected and "Battered Women," a video produced by Schuyler at the School of Social Work, was aired (unfortunately the authors have been unable to locate a copy of this video) Rain aided the effort. People rushed into the tent to get out of rain; 927 completed the survey. (Time Line/Wife Abuse) Parker and Dr. Roger Petersen, an assistant professor at the Research Center of the University of Maryland School of Social Work and Community Planning, analyzed the questionnaires completed by 311 men and 616 women. Data analysis revealed that 18% of women reported being "hit or beaten" by an intimate partner and 19% of men reported "slapping hitting or beating their wife or girlfriend." Of the abused women 92% of the black women and 83% of the white women said they would use the services of an emergency shelter. Finally, 65% of the men and 72% of women said they knew of a woman who had been abused. (Baltimore Report on Battered Women, page 3)

Participants were asked what they did following the abuse; a frequent response was "I cried." Although less scientifically valid than a later study by Hollander, Cohen, Associates (discussed below), responses from the City Fair survey provided task force members with effective anecdotes for later public speaking events.

In 1977, the Maryland Commission on Women and the Commission to Study Implementation of the Equal Rights Amendment, which Friedman chaired, joined forces to determine the extent of abuse in Maryland and the services needed by victims and perpetrators. With funding provided by the Department of Human Resources, the well-respected firm of Hollander, Cohen, Associates, Inc. conducted a random telephone survey in June 1977. Friedman acted as the project coordinator. Parker and Friedman, in consultation with Sidney Hollander, developed the questionnaire. Roger Peterson, Ph.D., from the School of Social Work, assisted in data analysis and writing the final report which was published in 1979 by the Department of Human Resources entitled "Inter-spousal Assault in Maryland." The original proposal was for a survey of both women and men; however, funding was cut and the final survey was limited to women. The goals of the study were to determine the incidence of violence between spouses in Maryland. Although the term "spouse" was used in the title of the study, one question determined the incidence of violence with someone with whom they had shared a household. The study did not include same sex or dating violence. (Friedman, Petersen, and Parker, 1979)

The study was significant as it used established scientific methodology to document the rates of spouse abuse in Maryland. This information was useful in later legislative initiatives including the legislation that led to funding of the House of Ruth. Because this kind of research study was relatively untested, the investigators decided to ask the telephone interviewers to provide their opinion of the respondent's attitudes regarding the questions. The choices included "interested and cooperative," "guarded or reluctant," and "suspicious, uneasy or hostile." Ninety-seven percent of the participants were described as "interested or cooperative;" 3% were judged to be "guarded or reluctant;" and less than 1% seemed "suspicious, uneasy or hostile."

As this was the first population-based study on family violence in Maryland, it was important to determine the rates of all forms of family violence. Therefore, the questionnaire asked the female participants about abuse to themselves as well as abuse they might have inflicted on their spouse or children. The interview questions differentiated between "hitting" and "abuse." "Spouse" was defined as "someone with whom they had cohabitated for at least a year." Finding from that study included the reported rates of being hit by one's husband and hitting the husband were at similar rates (16.5% vs. 16.2%);

The rates of "abuse" were 8.7% of women being abused vs. 2.0% of husbands abused and the rural Eastern Shore had the highest incidence of abuse, followed by Baltimore City.

These early research efforts set the groundwork of scientific evidence that helped in legislative and community efforts to develop a network of support for the establishment and later progress of the numerous shelter efforts. Additionally, the research findings provided important information when answering questions at later public appearances.

Questions from the Public

As part of Schuyler's mission to raise the issue "from the bottom up," speaking engagements were accepted (and solicited) from numerous community groups. This strategy of informing the public continued during the early years after the shelter was opened. In the May 1979 newsletter it is reported that in two months over 20 engagements were undertaken. In giving the lectures, the speakers learned to expect certain questions and comments. These included, "How do you know the women are telling you the truth and not exaggerating?" "I would never put up with that for one second" (always by a woman in the audience)"What about battered men?" and "Will women need to prove they are abused to use the shelter?"

One of Parker's "favorite" questions came from a reporter in Kansas City during a private interview who asked if women were hit while they were pregnant because they were a bigger target. To that question, Parker responded, "Maybe you should just let me talk and you can take notes."

In their responses, the speakers would emphasize that it would be unlikely that the women would be motivated to lie or exaggerate the abuse because there was nothing to gain. They pointed out the likelihood that there was an abused woman in the room at that moment, and that being unsympathetic to her would make her feel even more that she is crazy. Women put up with bad things for a lot of reasons such as for their children, their aging parents, and their belief that their husband is 'sick' or going through a bad time. Plus, abusers aren't *always* abusive; sometimes they are very loving and good providers also. Later, when psychologist Lenore Walker wrote about the stages of abuse, this answer incorporated her explanation of the cycle of violence. The speakers affirmed that there are indeed battered men and that shelters include provisions for them. Finally, they'd assert that there were no plans to ask women to show recent injuries to "prove" they had been abused.

Another frequent question was whether the speaker had a personal history of abuse. In answering this question, it was important to refrain from immediately saying "of course not," and to calmly explain how everyone has had an experience of being taken advantage of or not always taking care of themselves.

Statistical data, historical material and case anecdotes enhanced the ability to tell the story to the public. Getting the public's attention was only one piece of the plan. Organizing others to act together to bring about social change was the next step.

VI. Mobilizing Participants

In addition to getting the public's attention, advocates needed to reach out to motivate organizations, other professionals and citizens to support the cause and act. In keeping with the strategy of Brager and Sprecht, Schuyler proposed establishing "a network of motivated people who can inspire a change in services ... drawn from the target system itself: from social services, the police department and professionals who are linked to the problem." Schuyler struggled with the most effective approach, ultimately proposing the formation of a Battered Wives' Task Force comprised of representatives from social agencies and the community to suggest long-range planning alternatives and strategies for implementation. She recommended reaching out further to the police department, Court Commissioners' Office and other institutions such as Catholic Charities, Family and Children's Society, State's Attorney's Office, women's organizations and NOW. LAB would spearhead the formation of the task force. (Schuyler, 1975, p. 14-15)

Previous Community Efforts

Long before the volunteers adopted the social strategy/ community organization model, an early collaborative effort to address the issue of battered wives took place in 1970, beginning with a concern of a Baltimore City police officer about an overwhelming number of spousal assault cases being seen at one district station. A Northern Police District policewoman contacted the Greater Homewood Community Corporation (GHCC) seeking help with the serious problem of spousal assault with which she was dealing at the district building in Hampden. GHCC was a newly formed federation of community groups interested in improving the quality of life in north central Baltimore surrounding Johns Hopkins University. The policewoman's overriding concern was the "large number of families and couples who bring their domestic problems inappropriately to the district courts." The GHCC Family Services Committee (FSC) formulated a plan to study the extent of family violence reported to the Northern District and to recommend an intervention strategy. The committee proposed "a pilot program to demonstrate the need for specially trained counselors attached to district courts" to provide crisis intervention for abusers. (GHCC Minutes)

In January 1971, the FSC brought together a subcommittee of people with varied experiences to cross-pollinate ideas about how to address the problem and assist with finding project funding. The subcommittee included a municipal court judge, community representatives, and rep-

resentatives from the Bar Association of Baltimore City, the
Legal Aid Bureau, University of Maryland School of Social
Work, and police community relations. Virginia Magladery,
a supervisor at Family and Children's Society and the chair
of the FSC, knowing of Friedman's interest in battered
women, invited her to represent LAB on the subcommittee.
Efforts to obtain funding from Baltimore City and state
funding sources for the pilot program in the district court
were unsuccessful. The Department of Health and Mental
Hygiene and the Baltimore City Mayor's Office rejected the
proposed court counseling demonstration project. Likewise,
when the then-secretary of employment and social services
adopted and enlarged the project as a Court Domestic
Intervention and Pre-Trial Diversion Program, the governor
cut the allocated funds from the department budget.

The failure of GHCC's effort did not prove discouraging
to the LAB staff attorneys. The proposal had received
support from the chief judge of the District Court of
Maryland and the secretary of employment and social
services. The support of both was an encouraging sign. The
volunteer leaders continued to educate themselves about
the way women were treated and society's response and
moved forward with the Battered Women Project.

Parallel Efforts

Other women's organizations began to address
the problem. In 1975, the Maryland Commission on
the Status of Women (MCSW), operating under the

Maryland Department of Employment and Social Services, created a task force of women's groups to promote the establishment of a crisis shelter for battered women. Through a questionnaire, women's groups and social service agencies affirmed the need for a crisis shelter. (Time Line/Wife Abuse) The LAB joined the Task Force along with other organizations such as Associated Catholic Charities, Maryland Catholic Daughters of America, National Council of Jewish Women (NCJW), WISH, and Maryland Women Together.

Natalie (Toby) Mendeloff, who was a leader of WISH in the 1970s, agreed to be interviewed by the authors. In her 90s she remains stately in appearance with clear and articulate memories. She remembers the attractive Schuyler with her bright smile talking to them about homeless and battered women. Soon after, on a trip with her husband to Washington, D.C., Mendeloff visited the House of Ruth, a D.C. shelter established in 1976 for homeless women and children that also included battered wives. She reported what she learned there to the MCSW. (Mendeloff Interview)

The MCSW investigated possible sites, including a vacant West Baltimore convent and Baltimore City Hospitals in a section of C building, where abused women could be accommodated along with fire victims, people released from state institutions, and runaways. The group also researched funding resources, issuing a final report that declared a need for a crisis shelter but concluded a shelter could not be developed at the time. (Department of Human

Resources Proposal for Funding, Background, 1977) The
Health and Welfare Council of Central Maryland estimated
it would cost $275,000 for the first year. (Dickman) This
did not deter the effort to promote a crisis shelter. The
commission developed a comprehensive guide for groups
interested in establishing a shelter.

Shoshanna Cardin, the chair of the MCSW and a
well-known philanthropist and leader in the Jewish
community, and Ellen Moyer, executive director of the
MCSW (who later became mayor of Annapolis), gave
status and influence to the movement. Cardin began to use
the term "domestic violence." Friedman, concerned that
lumping battered women with child abuse could dilute the
understanding and impact of the social problem with which
adult women were dealing, objected to changing the phrase.
When mainstream publications and the legislative arena
chose to use the term "domestic violence," it became the
norm.

For the most part, the women involved in the
movement acted as consensus builders. Egos did flare
at times, especially when those working under the LAB
umbrella thought MCSW was taking credit for its efforts.
Eventually, Friedman confronted Cardin, reminding her
of the substantial amount of groundbreaking work that
had been done prior to its involvement. This cleared the
air and the groups worked together cooperatively and, in
the end, successfully. Schuyler observed, "By the time the
Commission threw its hat in the ring, the movement was

ready to expand to a statewide force and the Commission agreed to lend its resources to that effort. We appreciated them doing so." (Schuyler, Questionnaire)

Schuyler completed her field placement at LAB and coursework at the School of Social Work at the end of December 1975. At Friedman's urging, in January 1976, her work with the movement continued with the assistance of Lynn Deutschman. Back in 1973, Deutschman, a former teacher who was at home raising a child and needed some additional stimulation in her life, got involved through a personal encounter with an abused wife. Pizzey's work in London came to Deutschman's attention through an article she read that fascinated her.

"While reading this article, the phone rang and it was my husband. His secretary had come to work that day all battered, bruised and swollen. She was too embarrassed to talk to him and he asked if I would try and help her. … I called around to resources for her and everywhere I turned I heard the same story. 'We get requests for help all the time but don't have the wherewithal to help. Can you start something?' … I began planning how to educate agencies that have resources and funding but not the understanding of the problem." During my research I met Katy Friedman… (Deutschman Questionnaire)

Friedman, Schuyler and Deutschman met regularly to plan events and formulate ideas at Deutschman's Guilford home, often with Deutschman's fluffy white Bichon Frisé, Charlie, in attendance.

Community Support

Other organizations acted in concert with one another, planning and producing events all over Baltimore City and beyond. Schuyler's leadership resulted in Baltimore NOW sponsoring programs on the subject of battered women. The Legal Aid Bureau contributed panels at public events in this effort to get the word out. In February 1976, LAB and Baltimore NOW presented a panel discussion at the annual Women's Fair, sponsored by Baltimore Women Together, an umbrella organization of area women's groups–from the American Association of University Women to the Girl Scouts of Central Maryland to NOW. The all-day event took place at the Civic Center in Baltimore. (Women's Fair slated, *The Sun*) Numerous exhibitors from women's organizations, health groups, local colleges, government agencies and businesses participated. Workshops on various issues of interest to women, including "The Battered Women Syndrome," were featured. Deutschman coordinated arrangements for participating in the fair, including a booth to answer questions and hand out literature about the problem of battered women.

Collaboration

Among much collaboration, there was one between LAB and the Carruthers Center that deserves special emphasis. Carruthers is a mental health clinic in South Baltimore, and is part of the State Department of Health and Mental Hygiene. Schuyler successfully convinced the agency to work with LAB on services for battered women. Carruthers performed two important functions: keeping records that demonstrated the prevalence of domestic violence and starting the first hotline for battered women in Baltimore. (Schuyler Questionnaire Responses and Interview) Carruthers developed a coalition of service agencies and a network of services for battered women and their spouses. (Timeline/Wife Abuse)

The Caruthers Center participation led to the involvement of the Walter P. Carter Mental Health Center, a state-operated facility in existence at that time. In September 1976, the center opened a peer counseling service known as Battered Women's Anonymous. Marian Graham and Lois Mulder, psychiatric social workers, led the groups, which continued with the House of Ruth after its doors opened. (Department of Human Resources Proposal for Funding, Background, 1977) The Carter Health Center reported that 20 percent of its calls came from women complaining about spousal abuse. The figure increased to 70 percent after articles appeared in the newspapers and publication of the emergency service number. Barbara J. Parker assisted with the group in the absence of Graham or Mulder. (Battered Women: A Handbook)

> *Battered women would report that their husbands*
> *were extremely jealous and possessive. The*
> *woman was often forbidden from sitting on the*
> *stoop (a common summer activity prior to air*

conditioning), because passing men would look at
her.
> *– Barbara J. Parker, from Battered Women*
> *Anonymous.*

The year 1976 ended with the Maryland Conference
of Social Concern sponsoring a luncheon on the topic
"Battered Women: Protection and Solutions" at the Peabody
cafeteria on North Charles Street. *The Sun* announced
the conference in a November 30, 1976, article, identifying
Friedman and Schuyler as the speakers. ("Social concern
conference focuses on battered women," *The Sun*)

The activists were poised to energize the professional
and civic community to take action. The Maryland
Commission for Women (The former name, Maryland
Commission on the Status of Women, changed in 1976,
Chapter 119, Acts of 1976, Maryland Manual, 1989-1990, p.
315) had originated its own active engagement in the cause.
Now, all of the interested public and private organizations,
and community activists had to join in concerted action
focused on a specific goal around which all could rally—a
crisis shelter.

VII. Baltimore Task Force on Battered Women

It was Parker's suggestion to hold a symposium on the issue of battered women to explore the social, legal and psychological areas of wife abuse. LAB, Baltimore NOW and the Women's Law Center jointly planned and sponsored an all-day symposium at the University of Maryland School of Nursing on April 3, 1976. (Wife-Abuse Symposium Scheduled) Letters inviting participants were sent to local hospitals, social service agencies, criminal justice agencies and women's organizations. Local newspapers publicized the event. The goal of the educational forum was to draw more organizations and agencies into the movement through a task force to establish a shelter in Baltimore City. The number of people who attended, representing the health field, courts, police and psychiatric disciplines exceeded expectations.

The formal agenda included the videotape "Battered Women," produced by Schuyler, and an open discussion generated by the video. (Legal Aid Bureau, Inc., National Organization of Women, Women's Law Center Symposium on Battered Women Agenda and Evaluation) Friedman was also a keynote speaker. Having no budget for this meeting, the University of Maryland, School of Nursing graciously allowed the use of its entire building, and included paying for a security guard. To provide a coffee break the members all brought coffee pots from home. When they were all plugged in, a fuse was blown. Fortunately the security guard was able to locate and fix the problem.

A New Task Force

Out of the enthusiastic response to the symposium and the support of Baltimore NOW Study Committee for Battered Wives, the Baltimore Task Force on Battered Women was born in May 1976 to assist with the strategy developed by Schuyler to increase public awareness of the problem. The Task Force, at first a part of the Baltimore Chapter of NOW, had two primary goals: to educate the public and to advocate on behalf of battered women. Eventually, the participation broadened and the decision was made to establish the Task Force as a separate entity from Baltimore NOW. As stated in the Task Force bylaws, the primary goal of the newly organized task force was to mobilize agencies to provide services to victims of domestic violence in the areas of housing, law counseling, advocacy, and information and referral." (Department of Human Resources Proposal for funding, Background, 1977)

Brian Gamble, a University of Maryland social work student who had a passion for social causes (and was usually wearing overalls) became the chair of the Task Force, which included members representing the Maryland Catholic Daughters of America, Public Defenders Office, Carruthers Center, W.I.S.H, Displaced Homemakers, Salvation Army and the LAB. (See Appendix A for complete list) Through workshops and speaking engagements to community associations, philanthropic organizations, churches of all denominations, synagogues, colleges and universities, the City Fair, the Women's Fair—anywhere and everywhere they were welcome—the Task Force continued to spread the story, to educate the public, and to develop a public will to create a shelter.

Task Force speakers distributed "Battered Women: A Manual for Survival" authored by Friedman in 1976 for the Women's Law Center, a non-profit organization established in 1971, providing legal advocacy for women and children. This rudimentary pamphlet (the cover showing the face of a short-haired women with a fist smashed into the place where her nose would be), assembled in the mimeograph era, offered to battered women facts, practical advice and suggestions of where to go for help. The Task Force also prepared "Battered Women: A Handbook," full of background information to be used by speakers. This was a collaborative effort by Brian Gamble, Carolyn Rodis, Lois Hiemstra, Katy Friedman and Hazel Warnick. Parker created a bibliography to distribute as well.

Lynn Deutschman helped coordinate another program entitled "Battered Women: Catch 22" at the annual

Women's Fair in February 1977, attended by 2,000 people at the Poly-Western Complex in Baltimore. This program addressed the reason abused women stay with their mates and the lack of alternatives. (Brutality against wives linked to macho ethic, *The Sun*)

Public Television

During this period, Deutschman assisted in the production of a 90-minute Maryland Center for Public Broadcasting presentation on battered women. In a small ad in *The Sun,* the producer, Barbara Davis, announced, "… the intent is not to point up the problem further, but to explore avenues of treatment and to consider possible solutions." The ad resulted in a flood of telephone calls to the station, enabling them to interview close to 1,000 women. The producers conducted the interviews in motel rooms in neighborhoods scattered around the city. The findings were reported as part of a special called "The Battered Women" which aired February 20, 1977 on the station's four channels.

Deutschman made numerous public appearances, speaking to various audiences and television shows. Not everyone received the message agreeably. She recounts, "At one such [television] show, just as I was finished and we went to break, the camera man, a large angry fellow, approached me and began yelling that I had no right to tell him or anyone else how to treat his wife. He started grabbing me and they had to call security to pull him off. That only made me determined that more education was

needed." (Deutschman Questionnaire)

Through public announcements in local newspapers, the task force publicized its efforts to develop services for battered women, including counseling, legal aid and emergency shelter. (Help for battered women available, *The Sun*) Interest from the community and professionals was increasing. Momentum was building. The final push was near.

Sunpapers photos--Clarence B. Garrett and William H. Mortimer

BEATEN WOMAN ADVOCATES—Kathleen O'Ferrall Friedman, left, of Legal Aid Bureau, talks with client. She says many women complaining of wife beating end up staying with husband, lacking emotional strength or finances to leave. Delegate Pauline Menes, right, wants police to begin keeping statistics on domestic assaults to better define issue.

House of Ruth Maryland collection, Friedman papers.

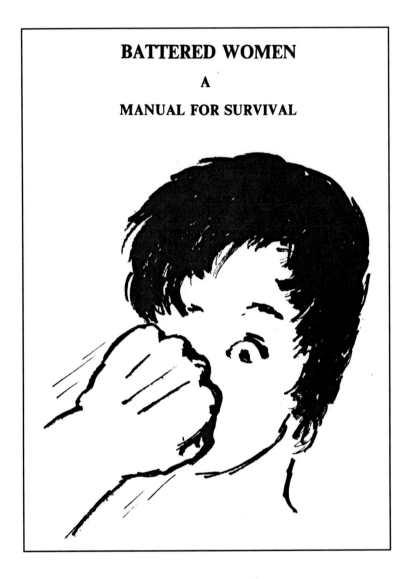

Cover to *Battered Women: A Manual for Survival*. Artwork by Dorothy Kerfoot. The Women's Law Center, 1976. *House of Ruth Maryland collection, Friedman papers.*

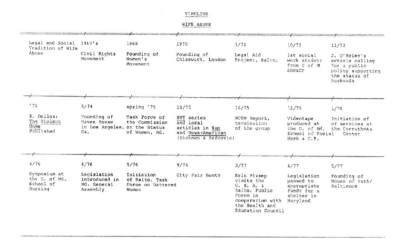

Timeline of the battered women's movement circa 1960s to 1977 prepared by Friedman and Schuyler. *House of Ruth Maryland collection, Friedman papers.*

Barbara J. Parker, a founding mother and Chair of the first House of Ruth Research Committee. *Parker family photograph.*

63

Natalie (Toby) Mendeloff, Women In Self Help. *Mendeloff family photograph*

Shoshana S. Cardin, Chair, Maryland Commission for Women. *Cardin family photograph.*

Lynn Deutschman, original member of the Baltimore Task Force
on Battered Women and volunteer coordinator for House of Ruth.
Deutschman family photograph.

Eva Barczak, former State Regent of Maryland Catholic Daughters
of America, was a "prime force" with the support of the Maryland
Commission for Women in opening the shelter. *House of Ruth Maryland
collection.*

Fights Battered Woman's Cause

Briton Tells Of London Shelter

By Sharon Dickman

Erin Pizzey has learned a lot about family violence from more than 7,000 battered women who have come to her women's shelter in London for help.

She is a plucky British woman who has attracted worldwide attention for the cause of women who are abused by their husbands or lovers.

So much attention, in fact, that she faces three months in jail because her Chiswick Women's Aid center never refuses a woman even when zoning regulations prohibit it.

"We are demanding national changes in thinking and policies and people, even if it means breaking the law," Mrs. Pizzey says about the need for shelters like hers. "England's answer to solving that problem is to take me to court."

She is visiting America for a few weeks to meet the many women who have written her about the need for services to battered women here. Mrs. Pizzey is baffled somewhat by America's bureaucracy and the talk she's heard while traveling about the difficulty in setting up shelters like her own.

"Do we really need lots and lots of [academic] papers or do we need shelters first and then the papers?" Mrs. Pizzey asked the audience at a conference on battered women yesterday at Essex Community College.

For several years, Baltimore women have been trying to get a shelter for homeless and battered women started, but with no real success. Part of that has to do with the fact that there does not seem to be anyone around quite like Erin Pizzey.

Kathleen O'Ferrall Friedman, a Legal Aid attorney, has worked several years with groups toward locating a house for the project, but has come up with nothing.

"We're all into our salaries, our jobs, our homes, our clothes. That's why we're not able to do this. We're in a real logjam, and I don't know what to do about it," Ms. Friedman admitted to the group. "We lack people like them."

But that talk isn't enough to dismay Mrs. Pizzey and the need she knows exists for women who have no place to go if they leave a violent situation at home.

"Chiswick isn't very expensive because professionals are our backups outside," she says about the operation she started in 1971. "They're there for us and we're there for these mothers."

Being *there* has often meant minimal or no salaries at all. Besides the primary center, she has also created a series of small 5-to-6 family community homes—where women pool their public assistance payments or whatever money they have—so women and their children can move after the initial adjustment period.

The legal requirement for her refuge is 36 persons, but Chiswick always houses many more than 100. The government is even withdrawing previous grants of more

than $20,000 to stop the overcrowding, which is an obvious sign of the continuing need.

Chiswick offers a home situation that might seem chaotic to some. Women and children sleep on mattresses with floor boards as their box springs. A filmed documentary on the shelter shows people coming and going, others cooking and cleaning and general mayhem.

"The first thing was that that many women together created a feeling of safety," she says of the value in such a group setting. "The chaos is very important because you're replacing one set of violence with a similar form of excitement, but a much more constructive one," the founder says.

"Some women are so broken down that they can hardly even organize a meal for their children, much less get up for work on time," says Mrs. Pizzey, a mother of two.

In Chiswick, there is no alcohol, no men and no violence permitted. The last one may be the hardest rule because many battered women thrive on violence, Mrs.

Pizzey has learned.

"Their pleasure and their pain seem very confused," she says of those women. All predictions are that battered children —male and female—grow up to do the same themselves.

Erin Pizzey's own mother was the victim of an abusive husband, she says, and the family's three children suffered the isolation even though they were not physically beaten.

In the film, Mrs. Pizzey talks about her mother's death from cancer and her father's refusal to bury her immediately.

"In his own way, he loved her passionately even though he mistreated her," says the 38-year-old Mrs. Pizzey.

The children were forced to watch their mother's body decompose for four days in the living room of their home before the burial finally took place.

"We were very frightened all the time," she says of that horrible account, "but no one would help us."

She doesn't want other women to feel that they are without help.

Sunpapers photo—George H. Cook

PLEADING FOR HELP—Erin Pizzey tells of setting up and operating her home for battered wives in London. She urged an Essex Community College crowd to help those persons who are trying to set up similar homes in this country.

House of Ruth Maryland collection, Friedman papers.

Baltimore, *Wednesday* THE EVENING SUN *October 12, 1977*

Homey Place In Charles Village

Refuge Near For Battered Women

By Ellen L. James

Baltimore's first shelter for battered women will open next month in a gray formstone rowhouse in Charles Village.

"When I walked in here, I just had a homey feeling, with those big windows and all the sun coming in." Marcella Schuyler, House of Ruth president, said recently as she wandered through the dusty, three-story building that will soon offer temporary housing for women beaten by their husbands.

"Chosing the location was difficult because we needed a place where black and white women would go, which was big enough, had low enough rent and where the community wasn't opposed to us," Ms. Schuyler said.

The house in the 2400 block Calvert street fills the bill, she said. It will open in about four weeks, after the refurbishing of the interior is complete, and will offer a hot-line, counseling and legal assistance.

"The emergency housing resources are just pitiful in this city," she said. Women who lack the $5 a night it costs to stay at the Salvation Army now sleep in abandoned houses, parks or the Greyhound terminal.

And the difficulty of finding money to flee from abusive husbands reaches middle-class women who often have no money for their own use.

"The problem cuts across socio-economic lines," Ms. Schuyler said. "It's not just a black women's problem. It's not a white women's problem. It's a women's problem."

The number of battered women leaving their husbands has increased threefold in the past few years as feminist thinking has spread. Today, women "realize they don't have to take it anymore and they're not the chattel of their husbands," Ms. Schuyler said.

She said that in the past humiliation and the scorn of society kept battered women from surfacing. "The message they got was, 'If your husband beats you, you deserve it'."

Even today, economic dependency and, in many cases, the threats of husbands who don't want their behavior exposed prevent such women from leaving the men who beat them.

Once they find the courage to go, "there's often a recuperative process. Women are devastated by the years of beating," according to Ms. Schuyler.

She said the aim of the House of Ruth will be to help its residents reorganize their lives and gain the independence to decide whether they want to keep their marriages. The house, she said, "won't take a stand as to whether they should split up or stay together."

Although there are no statistics available, Ms. Schuyler said she believes the abuse of women is "a serious problem" in Baltimore, judging from the reports of social welfare agencies and women who have reached out to her in desperation.

"For the women who are victims, it is a matter of life and death—it is that serious."

She anticipates that once House of Ruth is available it will be overwhelmed with women seeking its services. "The minute we open our doors, we're going to be inundated."

The abuse of women has long been a problem, she said, but was not widely recognized as such in the Baltimore area until feminist groups, such as the National Organization for Women, drew attention to it.

In January, 1976, NOW established a task force on battered women, which conducted a public information campaign. Ms. Schuyler, NOW's past president and a social worker with the city school system, was an active member of that task force.

Nine months later, the Baltimore Task Force on Battered Women was formed. Out of that group evolved the concept of creating a shelter, and a 20-member board was created to guide it.

Ms. Schuyler said it will cost about $50,000 for the shelter to operate in its first year. It now receives no government support, although it is seeking grants, and it has just enough money to stay afloat for the first three months.

The start-up money has come entirely through a series of small fund-raisers, pool and tennis parties held in August and September and from the organizers' pockets.

House of Ruth will hold a "housewarming dinner" October 22 at Notre Dame College and hopes to raise $1,500 through the event. Those who interested in attending the dinner should call Lynn Deutschman, 467-6738.

REFURBISHED SHELTER—Marcella Schuyler oversees the remodeling of a house in the 2400 block Calvert street that will be used as temporary refuge for battered women.

House of Ruth Maryland collection, Friedman papers.

First shelter at 2402 North Calvert Street, Baltimore.
House of Ruth Maryland collection.

Baltimore Report

on Battered Women

Issue 1   February, 1978

The Joint Publication of The House of Ruth, Baltimore, Inc. and The Baltimore Task Force on Battered Women.

Shelter Report

The long-awaited opening of the House of Ruth's Shelter at 2402 North Calvert Street finally occurred November 19, 1977. Since the opening, the shelter has been used by 44 women and 42 children. More women have come than children because some women have left their children with relatives while at the shelter and a few have had to leave in such a hurry that they've left their children at home.

Although exact statistics haven't yet been computed, it appears that the average length of stay has been about 10 days. Thus far the shelter Director reports that there have been no problems with angry husbands or with the women themselves physically disciplining, sometimes abusing their own children. Physical discipline of children is not allowed and the women have, after some initial reluctance, supported this rule very well.

Most of the women who have used the shelter have come from Baltimore City; most have been between ages 25 and 35. Black and white women have used the shelter in nearly equal numbers.

Residents of the shelter had a busy time during the holidays. Space was at a premium as requests for shelter seemed to multiply during the holiday season. Volunteers brought Thanksgiving dinner, Christmas decorations, and many toys for the children.

On January 10th, Congresswoman Barbara Mikulski visited the shelter to share dinner with residents and attend a Battered Women Together meeting. She discussed her new legislation (see Legislative Alert) with the battered women and asked for their input.

The house itself is being spruced up continually with the assistance of volunteers and residents. Windows are being caulked to keep out winter cold; laundry facilities are being put in working order, and home decoration continues.

NEWSFLASH!!!

The Mayor's Office of Manpower Resources has funded three CETA positions to expand the House of Ruth shelter staff. These positions — two counselors and a peer counselor — are expected to be filled by early March.

Introducing the Shelter Director

Dottie Benshoff is the first director of the House of Ruth's shelter. She is 36, has two teenage daughters, is separated, and has lived in Baltimore only six months.

Born and raised in North Bend, Ohio near Cincinnati, Dottie earned a B.A. in English at Millersville State College. Although she planned originally to teach after college, Dottie had some doubts after her student teaching experiences and instead decided to work for Pennsylvania's Mental Health and Mental Retardation Program (MHMR) in Lancaster, Pa. She started as an information referral caseworker and after 8 years had worked her way up to coordinator for services for children and youth. While working for MHMR Dottie became interested in the problem of wife beating and joined the coalition of women that eventually opened a shelter for battered women in the Lancaster area in 1976. She was an active volunteer in this shelter until her move to Baltimore in August 1977.

Asked about her experiences with the Calvert Street shelter, Dottie said, "Its been terrific. The women and I have been learning a lot from each other."

Special Events

February

| 15 Annapolis | Legislative Coalition sponsored by the Maryland Commission for Women. For information, call 383-5608 |
| date uncertain | February meeting of the Baltimore Task Force on Battered Women. To get meeting date and time, call Brian Gamble at 727-7777. |

March

| 16 | Family Violence Conference. Essex Community College - Lecture Hall 9 a.m. to 4 p.m. Speaker - Dr. Susan Steinmetz, Ph.D. To Register - Call Joanna Franklin 686-3610 |

Baltimore Report on Battered Women, Issue 1, February 1, 1978 – first House of Ruth newsletter (page 1 of 4) *Health and Welfare Council of Central Maryland Archives, University of Baltimore.*

Top two women, left to right: Joyce Kroeller and Kathleen Ellis, former
House of Ruth presidents, with three volunteers, 1978.

HOUSE OF RUTH

Crisis Shelter Program for Battered Women

- SHELTER IN A FRIENDLY, HOMELIKE ATMOSPHERE
- 24-HOUR TELEPHONE COUNSELING
- 24-HOUR INFORMATION AND REFERRAL
- INDIVIDUAL, COUPLE AND GROUP COUNSELING
- ADVOCACY FOR BATTERED WOMEN AND THEIR CHILDREN
- COMMUNITY EDUCATION AND INFORMATION
- COUNSELING AND SHELTER, IF NEEDED, FOR BATTERED MEN
- INDIVIDUAL AND GROUP COUNSELING FOR BATTERERS

SERVICES ARE PROVIDED FOR BOTH SHELTER AND NON-SHELTER CLIENTS
IF YOU WANT MORE INFORMATION OR NEED HELP,
PLEASE CALL 889 - RUTH.

What is the House of Ruth?

The House of Ruth was organized in the Spring of 1977 by representatives of various women's groups and other individuals concerned with the problems of domestic violence. The House of Ruth opened its doors in November, 1977, and since that time has provided shelter and counseling to battered women and their children.

The purposes of the House of Ruth are (1) to provide a sheltered environment, guidance, and supportive services to meet the special needs of battered women and their children and (2) to provide community education and information regarding the problems of battered women.

What you can do to help...

To continue to provide services to battered women and their children, The House of Ruth must depend - to a great extent - on fundraising, on donations, and on volunteers. Donations of money, food and household items are accepted. Volunteers are needed to answer the telephone, to provide transportation, to take care of the children, and to help with many other activities of the House. If you can help in any way, please call 889-RUTH.

In 1978...

the House of Ruth provided shelter to 217 women and 270 children.

DISPOSITION		LENGTH OF STAY		RACE	
(July 1-December 31)		1-5 days	92	100 Black Women	
28 Returned to husband		6-10 days	40	108 White Women	
7 Returned home with-		11-15 days	28	9 Other	
out husband		16-30 days	26		
32 Established new		61 & over	12	AGE	
residence		not available	19	19 or less	15
26 Moved in with relatives				20-29	122
19 Moved in with friends		GEOGRAPHIC LOCATION		30-39	58
3 Went to hospital		161 Baltimore City		40-49	16
3 Obtained live-in position		27 Baltimore County		50-59	3
2 Asked to leave		16 other Maryland		60 & over	1
5 Unknown		13 unknown		unknown	2

P.O. Box 7276 ● Baltimore, Maryland ● 21218

A 1978 House of Ruth flyer describing the services offered at the House of Ruth. *Health and Welfare Council of Central Maryland Archives, University of Baltimore.*

In 1978... the House of Ruth provided shelter to 217 women and 270 children.

DISPOSITION	LENGTH OF STAY		RACE	
(July 1-December 31)	1-5 days	92	100 Black Women	
28 Returned to husband	6-10 days	40	108 White Women	
7 Returned home with-	11-15 days	28	9 Other	
out husband	16-30 days	26		
32 Established new	61 & over	12	AGE	
residence	not available	19	19 or less	15
26 Moved in with relatives			20-29	122
19 Moved in with friends	GEOGRAPHIC LOCATION		30-39	58
3 Went to hospital	161 Baltimore City		40-49	16
3 Obtained live-in position	27 Baltimore County		50-59	3
2 Asked to leave	16 other Maryland		60 & over	1
5 Unknown	13 unknown		unknown	2

Description of clients served in 1978. *Health and Welfare Council of Central Maryland Archives, University of Baltimore.*

Councilwoman Mary Pat Clarke and Representative Barbara A. Mikulski (now a U.S. Senator) at a House of Ruth reception in 1978. *House of Ruth Maryland collection*

HOUSE OF RUTH

newsletter
MAY, 1979

The House of Ruth cordially invites you to attend its annual meeting on May 21, 1979, at 7:30 p.m., in Fourier Hall at Notre Dame College, North Charles Street at Homeland Avenue. New officers and board members will be elected. Kathleen O'Ferrall Friedman will be the guest speaker. Refreshments will be served after the meeting. Please join us.

COUNSELING GROUPS

The House of Ruth now provides services to violent spouses and couples with domestic violence problems. Two counselors, Ned Green and Fran Fitch, have been hired on a part-time basis to provide these new services. The couple counseling began the middle of March, and the first group for batterers will begin May 15. More information can be obtained by calling the House of Ruth at 889-RUTH.

CONGRESSIONAL LEGISLATION

Representative Miller of California and fifty other legislators have introduced H.R. 2977, the Domestic Violence Prevention and Services Act, to provide funding for state, local, and community programs and activities pertaining to domestic violence. This bill, if passed, would authorize $65 million over three years, 75% of which would be marked for the operation of crisis shelters. Hearings are expected to be held in late May. Please write to your Congressional representatives to urge their support of this bill. Also, please write to Representative Paul Simon, chairperson of the subcommittee which will have hearings on this bill, to urge prompt scheduling of the hearings. Address your letters to:

Rep. Paul Simon, Chairperson
Select Education Subcommittee
Education and Labor Committee
House of Representatives
Washington, D. C. 20515

CAN YOU HELP?

Volunteers are needed to help in all phases of the House of Ruth program. Some of the activities include: telephone counseling; transportation; child care; on-call at night; fundraising; speakers bureau; and staffing of booths at fairs. We have a current need for volunteers to drive our house manager and a resident to do the weekly grocery shopping. If you can do this on a weekly, bi-monthly, or a monthly basis (or even just once) call Joan at the House.

Crisis Shelter Program for Battered Women • P.O. Box 7276 • Baltimore, Maryland • 21218

1979 House of Ruth Newsletter with early logo. *Health and Welfare Council of Central Maryland Archives, University of Baltimore.*

A BENEFIT FOR THE **HOUSE OF RUTH**

Skateland
(next to Painters Mill Music Hall)

Skate-A-Thon

THE LONGER YOU ROLL, THE MORE MONEY YOU HELP RAISE FOR THE HOUSE OF RUTH

November 5, 1979   5 p.m. to 10 p.m.

TICKETS: $5.00 – Children under 14 years of age admitted free with pledge cards.
(skate rentals – 75¢)

CELEBRITY SKATERS ✳ WHEELS OF CHANCE AND GAMES ✳ REFRESHMENTS AVAILABLE

FOR TICKETS AND PLEDGE CARDS – CALL 889-6679

HOUSE
OF RUTH

CRISIS SHELTER PROGRAM FOR BATTERED WOMEN

Box 7276 ● Baltimore, Maryland 21218 ● 889-RUTH

Fundraiser flier for Skate-A-Thon, November 1979; original in bright
green and blue. *House of Ruth Maryland collection.*

Karen Kelley's strong administrative abilities promoted early stability.
In 1978, she became the second president of House of Ruth Maryland.
House of Ruth Maryland collection.

Help For The Battering

HOUSE OF RUTH
P.O. Box 7276
Baltimore, Maryland 21218

And Abusive Spouse

• Crisis Counseling (24 HOUR HOTLINE)
889-7884

• Group Counseling • Couples Counseling

THE HOUSE OF RUTH is now adding a new program of services to the abusive and battering spouse. The addition to our present program of shelter, counseling and supportive services for battered and abused spouses is made in recognition of the need for a comprehensive approach to the problem of domestic violence.

THE BATTERING AND ABUSIVE SPOUSE PROGRAM HAS THREE PRIMARY COMPONENTS:

Crisis intervention with the batterer. This service is available 24 hours daily by calling the House of Ruth hotline. (889-7884). Intervention will include assessment of the crisis, planing and action for its resolution, support during the crisis, and referral to other services as needed.

Short-term counseling with couples in battering/abusive crisis. Counseling with couples will be limited to a 6 week period with resolution of the battering crisis as the goal. If continued services are needed after the crisis period, referral will be made to the appropriate family service or mental health resource.

Group Therapy for the batterer. Group therapy will be provided as an on-going, long-term service of the program. Group participants will have the opportunity to share and learn from each other, to give and receive support in their efforts to change themselves, and to become aware of the attitudes, feelings and situations that contribute to their battering behavior. Clearly the goal of such groups will be to enable the participants to learn and use effective, constructive, satisfying alternatives to their previous destructive behavior. Persons seeking the services of this program will be screened and evaluated prior to inclusion in group therapy.

Referrals to this program will be accepted from anyone who believes that they or someone they know has a problem with spousal abuse, as well as from judicial, law-enforcement, social and medical agencies or private practitionors. Referrals or inquiries may be made by calling 889-7884.

A New Service Of The House Of Ruth
If you want more information or need help, please call **889-RUTH.**

This 1979 flyer promoted services available for abusive spouse. *Health and Welfare Council of Central Maryland Archives, University of Baltimore.*

77

Former presidents of the House of Ruth in the early years. Left to right
Marilyn Maultsby, Marcella Schuyler, Jodi Dunn,and Carole Maier.
House of Ruth Maryland collection.

The authors (left, Friedman and right, Parker) posed after interviewing
Marcella Schuyler (center), first president of the House of Ruth, Sarasota
Florida in May 2013. *Parker family photograph.*

VIII. The House of Ruth Is Born

It became clear through conferences and articles
appearing in popular magazines that other places in
the state and nation were establishing shelters. With the
Washington, D.C. House of Ruth as a model, and with
help from the founder of the D.C. shelter, volunteer Eva
Barczak (Mrs. Joseph A. Barczak) began pressing forward
on identifying a location for a crisis shelter. Barczack was
a member of MCW, representing the Maryland Catholic
Daughters of America, of which she had been a past state
regent. *The Sun* reported her numerous efforts. Clearly an
action-oriented person, even in her 80s, and with close ties
to the Catholic Dioceses, she located the then-vacant St.
Anne's parish house on Greenmount Avenue as a possible
shelter site. Not to be deterred by the lack of financing,
Barczak went so far as to take a 60-day option on the house
in hopes of getting financial support. She suggested, "There
is certainly enough evidence that we need this house. The
idea is to get all the women's groups to support this project.
If we could get enough money pledged for six months, we
could get going. If every group could give something, then

we could get started." (Henderson, 1977)

Critical Conferences

In an effort to generate support, in mid-March 1977, the Maryland Commission for Women, together with College of Notre Dame of Maryland (now Notre Dame of Maryland University) sponsored a conference to reexamine the possibility of establishing a crisis shelter for battered women and their children. Out of this conference grew a substantial group of women willing to dedicate themselves to the founding of the shelter. Randi Henderson reported in *The Sun*, Wednesday, March 23, 1977, "The result of that conference was the establishment of an ad hoc committee to work on establishing a shelter." (Henderson, 1977)

The following week, on March 29, the Baltimore Task Force on Battered Women, Maryland NOW, in cooperation with the Health and Welfare Council of Central Maryland, (The Health and Welfare Council, a planning, coordinating and research agency, was succeeded by the Maryland Association of Nonprofit Organizations in 1992) joined forces to sponsor a one-day educational forum for workers in the field and the public at Essex Community College (Henderson, 1977) The program included a keynote speaker in the morning and five workshops in the afternoon conducted by medical and legal professionals. (Program on battered women, *The Sun*)

Erin Pizzey

The program attracted "more than 100 persons from the

legal, medical and social services fields." (Worobec) At the suggestion of Barbara J. Parker and Lynn Deutschman, the keynote speaker was Erin Pizzey. She had been planning a trip to the United States and added Baltimore to her itinerary. The Salvation Army had sponsored her national trip to inspire the development of shelters in the United States.

Her inspiring talk was comprised primarily of a film of her traumatic childhood and efforts to intervene on behalf of battered women. "The film about Chiswick shows women arriving at the shelter, the daily activities there, children at the day school, and group sessions." ("Ms. Steinem to Host 'Tragedy of Battered Wives'," 1977) Pizzey noted that there were empty, boarded-up homes in Baltimore City and recommended that the Task Force find a group of women and children and take over these empty properties. Call the newspapers, she suggested, so that there will be reporters and cameras to take pictures of the women and children being evicted. Pizzey, described by one newspaper as "plucky," gave a rousing speech, urging those present to "just do it." The task force did "do it," but in a decidedly more legal fashion, probably because many lawyers were involved in the effort.

On the day of the program, Task Force members met the train when Pizzey and three colleagues arrived from New York. As she departed from the train, her first words were. "Hello dearies, Can we go find a small drinky?" Task Force members quietly shared looks with each other concerned

about keeping her sober (Pizzey later published a book
where she frankly discussed her issues with mental illness
and alcoholism) Again working on a shoestring, Task Force
members hosted the four visitors in their homes.

That same night, the Baltimore Task Force on Battered
Women sponsored Pizzey at College of Notre Dame of
Maryland where she again showed her film about battered
women and gave a talk about the London shelter. The
program was preceded by a buffet dinner, costing $25,
hosted by the then-president of the college Kathleen Feeley,
SSND. (Schuyler Interview)

Ad Hoc Action

These events hastened establishment of the crisis shelter.
The ad hoc committee, 25 women infused with enthusiasm
and tenacity, comprised the core group that took the basic
steps of creating the non-profit organization, which opened
a shelter later that year. (See Appendix C) The shelter was
the outgrowth of the efforts of 12 organizations: Baltimore
NOW, Baltimore Task Force on Battered Women, Catholic
Daughters of America, Displaced Homemakers, Legal
Aid Bureau, MCW, Maryland Women Together, National
Council of Jewish Women, New Directions for Women,
Women in Self Help (WISH), Women's Law Center, Inc. and
the Women's Resource Center. In a multitude of ways, these
organizations were the impetus to get the job done. This
Task Force demonstrated the old adage: success has many
mothers, while failure is an orphan.

The ad hoc committee met regularly at the Govans United Methodist Church in the 5200 block of York Road to establish the organization, which all agreed should be named The House of Ruth, Baltimore, Inc. Both Toby Mendeloff and Eva Barczak, by now members of the *Ad Hoc* Committee, championed the name "House of Ruth," which was appealing because of the Biblical story of Ruth.

When Naomi, an Israelite, loses her husband and sons, her non-Israelite daughter-in-law Ruth vows to stay with her –"… where you go I will go, and where you lodge I will lodge. …," The Book of Ruth 1:15

They and other members of the ad hoc committee saw the D.C. shelter as an inspiration. Schuyler remembers doing a radio interview where a call-in person asked if we used the name "House of Ruth" because Babe Ruth was such a good slugger. "In the end it was fortunate we did not have any big benefactors who needed to be honored with the naming because 'House of Ruth' has served us well," she observed. (Schuyler Interview)

The ad hoc committee, working diligently, addressed organizational matters, governance, funding and location of a facility. It established its mission, legal status as a corporation, by-laws and the governing Board. With Friedman acting as "pro bono" counsel, the committee approved Articles of Incorporation and by-laws, which set forth the mission of the organization and its administrative structure. A not-for-profit corporation, Article III(1) establishes the primary purpose to "secure, establish and

maintain one or more shelters for homeless, destitute
and battered women. The first shelter shall serve battered
women." Other stated purposes include: "to provide
intervention and supportive counseling, to collect and
compile statistics, and to improve community understanding
of the causes of homeless, destitute and battered women."
(Articles of Incorporation) Incorporating provided a
legal entity to conduct business and gave credibility to
the nascent organization. It also protected the board of
directors from personal liability. As of July 7, 1977, the State
Department of Assessments and Taxation approved the
Articles of Incorporation of The House of Ruth, Baltimore,
Inc. Friedman continued as a volunteer legal advisor to the
shelter in its early years.

Efforts to plan the opening of the shelter, hiring staff
and operating the home were in full swing, but developing
a fundraising base in the community proved difficult
without tax exempt status. Obtaining recognition of such an
exemption was a priority to enable successful fundraising,
particularly related to grants and monetary gifts from
foundations. Friedman drafted and filed application for tax
exempt status as a charitable organization. The Internal
Revenue Service later certified the House of Ruth's
non-profit status as a 501 (c) (3) organization.

Fundraising

Funding the program was a major issue, causing a great
deal of discussion and hand wringing. On her way to one

of the ad hoc committee meetings, Eva Barczak raised the
first $5. Crossing the street, she ran into another Catholic
Daughters member. She told her about what the House of
Ruth was trying to do and asked for money. Waving the $5
bill to those present at the meeting, she proudly announced
her achievement. Schuyler recognizes Barczak as a prime
force, a "pusher," someone with a lifetime of experience
who showed the activists the way. Praising Barczak, Schuyler
commented, "She was eager to have something to show for
her involvement. If we waivered about moving forward,
she would push the conversation forward and show little
tolerance for ambivalence. After all, God was on her side.
The lesson we learned from Eva was 'just ask.'" (Schuyler
Interview) The cause was worthy; the money would come.
The volunteers' youth and zeal propelled them forward.
Early funding came from individuals as a result of numerous
private dinners and parties, as well as telephone solicitations.

A 20-member board of directors was formed from
the ad hoc committee and officers were elected. Marcella
Schuyler became the first president. The other founding
officers were Katie Ryan, vice president, Audrey Harris,
secretary, and Elizabeth Stanford Butterfield, treasurer.
Schuyler, Ryan and Harris were the original signers of the
Articles of Incorporation.

Having completed social work school, and now at the
end of her term as president of Baltimore NOW, and with a
young child, Schuyler was tired and meeting-weary. By her
own admission, she was acutely aware of her own deficits,

did not know how to fundraise, did not know people with money, had no experience with the public sector, had only fledging organizational skills, and needed to work full time. Nevertheless, she reluctantly agreed to Friedman's exhortation that she accept the presidency. (Schuyler Interview) Friedman knew that Schuyler underestimated her skills and that it was crucial to the first year of operation to have a proven leader who brought passion to the effort.

IX. First Year

One of the hardest tasks Schuyler had as president was trying to get a divergent group of women to work together. With laughter, she paints a picture of the gatherings:

Imagine the following: at one meeting we might have an 80-year-old Catholic Daughter with a kerchief holding her hair in place, a 60s jean feminist lesbian who could swear like a trouper, a housewife from suburbia, professionals. Meetings were so raucous that I remember (with embarrassment) using a bell to get order. Roberts Rules of Order you say? Well, those were way too establishment, and furthermore, I would have needed to spend time learning them and every minute was taken. (Schuyler Questionnaire)

A Building

The House of Ruth board began looking for a building to accommodate a shelter in Baltimore City. Schuyler recounted that looking for a building took many site visits and a good stomach, which limited the searchers to certain board members who could handle the "surprises." She recalled, "We went into buildings that had dirty mattresses on the floor with drunks and stoned teenagers. Rats were not unusual. Realtors saw a chance to unload undesirable property. When we came upon the Calvert Street property, we saw a building that was not too large to renovate but had enough small rooms to accommodate us." (Schuyler Interview)

> *When I rang the doorbell at the House of Ruth*
> *and someone let me in I said, "Am I home?" and*
> *she said yes— the end of the trip which could*
> *have lasted a few blocks or a hundred miles. This*
> *place, never seen before, represented safety from*
> *an intolerable situation.*
> *– Shelter Resident, Let Her Voice Be Heard, p. 4*

On November 19, 1977, the shelter, which could accommodate 15 women and children at a time, opened at 2402 North Calvert Street, a gray Formstone row house in Charles Village, described in one newspaper article as a "nine room house, one of the block's vintage buildings with its 10-foot-high ceilings and bay windows." (Pawlyna, 1978) The rent was $125 per month, and initially, the location was kept confidential. In a column in *The Evening Sun,* Schuyler was quoted as saying, "Choosing the location was difficult because we needed a place where black and white women would go, which was big enough, had low enough rent and where the community wasn't opposed to us." (James, 1977) Volunteers helped scrub and clean the shelter before

it was occupied. Deutschman, at this time the volunteer
coordinator, recalls,

> We scrubbed and cleaned and painted this house. …
> We needed everything from toothbrushes and clothing to
> furniture and food. … We had advocates to take women
> through the legal process, and to work with the children.
> And we had wonderful volunteers to help women get back
> their dignity and self-respect. We identified apartments
> that were affordable as well as adequate for a family of
> at least four and helped women find employment. It was
> never enough, but it was a wonderful beginning. Many of
> our volunteers were formerly battered women themselves.
> (Deutschman Questionnaire)

Community and Professional Support

No sooner had the shelter opened its doors when
the Soroptimist International of Baltimore sponsored a
Christmas party. Its project was to donate a clothes washer
to the House of Ruth. (Club plans Christmas party, *The Sun*)
In a response to a feature article in *The Sun*, the shelter
received cash donations, household items and volunteer
assistance. The initial staff consisted of some 30 volunteers.
The Baltimore Report on Battered Women noted that
members of the Baltimore Task Force remained "deeply
involved in getting the House of Ruth off the ground." For
example, Lois Hiemstra took the time to develop a resource
file to be used by residents. And both she and Brian Gamble
relieved Benshoff, who at the time was the only employee.

(Baltimore Report on Battered Women, p. 3)

Schuyler was good at identifying people who were willing to help and who had the skills to move the program forward. One of her backups was Karen Kelley, a Johns Hopkins School of Hygiene and Public Health graduate, a systems thinker with good negotiations skills. Schuyler described Kelley this way: "Karen had very good administrative skills and won many arguments with people who were blocking our path. ... Karen is one of those people who were always 'cool' and attracted people in a very natural way because of her self-confidence and fun-loving personality." Kelley later became the second president of the House of Ruth. She brought in a volunteer tax lawyer to set up proper bookkeeping, "which allowed [the shelter] to grow from a shoe-box accounting system to something that could actually pass the auditor's review." Schuyler learned organizational and public relations skills and gained a track record, but most of all, she came to appreciate that every person could bring something of value to the effort. (Schuyler Interview)

The board hired the first executive director in 1978. Dottie Benshoff was a transplant from Lancaster, Pa., where she had joined a coalition that opened a shelter. She set up routines to organize the house. In an extensive article appearing in *The Sunday Sun* on January 1, 1978, Benshoff described the counseling offered as "tailored to each woman" and, for women who were beyond reconciliation with their mates, the shelter acted as a clearinghouse referring divorce matters to Legal Aid and applications for housing and welfare to the Department of Social Services. Assistance finding jobs was channeled through New Directions for Women, a non-profit employment counseling center, and the Displaced Homemaker Program, which specialized in placing women older than 35 years. (Pawlyna, 1978)

The newspaper article included discussion of some house policy. Length of stay was flexible, but, generally, two months was considered the maximum. Nominal fees were charged only when appropriate.

The women are expected to divide up household chores and run the house together. They need observe only a few rules: a 10 p.m. daily curfew; no drugs or alcohol; no visits from the spouse or boyfriend who beat them; and no violent behavior (such as spanking or excessive shouting) toward their children. (Pawlyna, 1978)

Growth

During the first month, the program sheltered 12 women and 11 children. By the end of February 1978, the House of Ruth had admitted 41 women (not counting children), having to turn away another 47 women. The program had 40 volunteers to assist the one full-time employee. In a newspaper article, Schuyler was quoted as saying, "It's hard to run a 24-hour-a-day service with just one paid staff member." Early in the program it was costing $2,000 a month to run the program, but Schuyler envisioned a "first-rate refuge" costing about $100,000 a year." (Price, 1978) Schuyler noted, "The demand for service was so great that we have turned away more women than we have been able to help." (Schuyler, Untitled and undated comments to a public gathering, probably in 1978) A newspaper column in late February reported that the shelter might have to close unless people responded to Schuyler's plea for contributions, pending state and federal funding. (Women's shelter could close, *The Sun*)

Many women's groups answered the call. The Women's Council of Realtors, National Association of Realtors sponsored a buffet dinner and play at the Limestone Valley Theatre. Among the beneficiaries of the proceeds was the House of Ruth. (Dinner theatre trip set, *The Sun*) Likewise, the Towson State University Women's Center sponsored a food drive to support the shelter. (Food drive set up for House of Ruth, *The Sun*)

Many social service agencies assisted the startup. The Maryland Food Committee provided a grant to cover initial food expenses. Associated Catholic Charities supplemented the minimal staff by lending a social worker one day a week until the end of the year (1978) Brian Gamble, who chaired the Baltimore Task Force on Battered Women, was that social worker, making it possible for the director to take off one day a week. (Baltimore Report on Battered Women)

City departments aided the cause. Mayor William Donald Schaefer ordered the city's civil defense office to provide blankets for the shelter. (Price, 1978) The Mayor's

Office of Human Resources helped with administrative issues. The Director of the Baltimore City Department of Social Services (DSS) agreed that DSS would cooperate wherever possible (Baltimore Report on Battered Women) After retiring, Esther Lazarus, who had been director of DSS from 1953 to 1968, helped found WISH and became a board member of the House of Ruth. (Esther Lazarus, welfare chief of city until 1968, dies at 80, The Sun) The State's Attorney for Baltimore City by memorandum officially recognized the problem of battered women. (Time Line/Wife Abuse)

Funding remained a challenge, which caused the board much anxiety. Initial funding came through cash and in-kind contributions from private sources. Individuals, women's groups, churches and professional groups contributed money, furniture, housewares, clothing and toys. In February 1978, Schuyler reported that the start-up money came entirely through a series of small fundraisers and from the organizers' pockets. (James, 1977) Cash contributions came mostly in sums of $5 to $25. (Baltimore Report on Battered Women) Schuyler laughs when recounting the first big fundraiser — a Champagne Cruise on the Port Welcome in June 1978 that she dubbed "The Titanic." The tickets were a hard sell. (Schuyler Interview) Yet, the House of Ruth continued its growth, attracting more volunteers and donors.

Volunteers and Donors

A neighbor showed Judith (Judy) Katz an article about the House of Ruth in a local paper. A stay-at-home mom with a master's degree in library science, Katz had two small children, one an infant. Katz puzzled about why the neighbor suggested that she get involved as a volunteer, but decided to offer her help. (Katz Questionnaire) She is typical of many of the volunteers that assisted the program. She turned out to be an organizational whiz. "Until we found Judy Katz, our organizational minutes were hit and miss. ... Some tasks that today are trifling were monumental because of the lack of technology and resources. To manage our ever-growing mailing list, which demanded accuracy, was essential." (Schuyler Interview)

Katz tells a story related to her task of acknowledging contributions. It is a snapshot of the individuals who gave small amounts of money.

> *We started to get donations on a monthly basis from a woman. These were usually $44 but very occasionally they were $55. I wrote thank you after thank you to her, and finally curiosity got the better of me and I inquired in one of my letters what prompted the monthly donation and the amount of these donations. Her response was that she had been hospitalized and had gotten no communication from her church while she was in hospital except for a dunning letter about the church building fund. Hurt, she decided to donate what had been her weekly church donation to the House of Ruth. So $11 a week came from her to us.*

One story Schuyler tells shows the unexpected things that happened from time to time. A woman came to the shelter with her children. She was quite a talker who reacted strongly to what she saw, exclaiming, "Look at all these women and children, and they are hungry, and my husband owns a bakery." She used the telephone to call her husband. "You want me back, you deliver bread here," she demanded. Her husband delivered the bread. (Schuyler Interview)

Toby Mendeloff brought one of the first potential major donors to the table (literally) to meet for lunch with Schuyler at the Charles Street house. While Schuyler was making her pitch for funds, the chair on which the potential donor was sitting began to groan and collapse from under her. With no harm done, Schuyler survived this embarrassment to retell the story many times. (Schuyler Interview)

Volunteers at the shelter never knew what to expect. Parker has a memory of the smoke alarms going off so frequently that the women would remove the batteries. Putting a lot of women and children in a small space meant that there were often colds and other illnesses among the residents. This was often the result of a new environment with unfamiliar people, compounded by the stress of dislocation and recovering from violence. Lice were also an issue. When their children became sick, some women felt guilty about taking them from their home.

As a nurse, Parker was concerned with food spoilage and contamination. Some new mothers would reuse the same bottle of formula for their baby the entire day without refrigeration. There was also a fair amount of gastrointestinal distress that Parker attributed to dishes not being properly sanitized. By the time the House of Ruth moved to the second shelter, Parker was able to convince people that a dishwasher was not a luxury but a necessity with so many people sharing food and utensils. Even then, it was not unusual for a woman to hand wash dishes saying "it is no bother for these few items."

> *One woman reported being attacked with a knife*
> *when she refused sexual intercourse three days*
> *following a hysterectomy. As a nurse, I learned*
> *that I needed to ask about potential problems*
> *when talking to women about required sexual*
> *abstinence.*
> *– Barbara J. Parker*

Schuyler worried that talking about the lack of money with the media could backfire. But publicity about the need for operating funds and in-kind contributions worked. (Schuyler Questionnaire) Various organizations sponsored food drives and dance marathons to help with expenses. By the end of 1977, the House of Ruth raised more than $12,000. Contributions from individuals, church groups and other organizations amounted to $6,415.46. Fundraising events gleaned $5,346 and one grant provided $500. With expenses of a little over $5,300, the first financial statement

showed a fund balance of almost $6,900 which carried
over to the next year. (The House if Ruth, Baltimore, Inc.
Operating Statement, December 31, 1977)

In February 1978 the first newsletter was published
and included a report on the number of people receiving
services, a summary of current legislation proposed, a
call for volunteers and the results from the 1976 City Fair
survey. It also included a tear-off form for contributions that
noted that a donation of $5.00 included membership in the
"Friends of the House of Ruth."

X. Law and System Reform Efforts

The LAB, the Governor's Commission to Study
the Implementation of the Equal Rights Amendment,
Maryland NOW, MCW and the Women's Law Center
promoted legislation to provide protection against domestic
violence and lobbied extensively for its passage. Early
efforts were unsuccessful. The 1976 General Assembly of
Maryland considered a number of bills addressing battered
women. Prince George's County Delegate Pauline Menes,
a champion of protection for battered wives, sponsored
House Joint Resolution 78 of the General Assembly which
would have required police departments in Maryland
to keep statistics on the incidence of domestic assault. It
failed to pass. (Dickman) A bill seeking record keeping by
the State Police of the incidence of inter-spousal violence
failed. At the request of the LAB, the Baltimore City Police
Department collected data showing the high incidence of
assaults, especially aggravated assault between spouses.
Legislation on inter-spousal immunity (House Bill 124)
failed. Also, Senate Bill 442 to remove the family exclusion
from the Criminal Injuries Compensation Act failed.

Success

One victory occurred in 1976, when the General Assembly passed an emergency measure to protect any party to an action for divorce, alimony or annulment from physical harm or harassment of any kind by granting a court of equity the power to exclude a party from the family home or from the home of the other party. (*Battered Women: A Handbook*, p. 22)

That same year, the LAB successfully negotiated standards of procedure in handling complaints of inter-spousal violence with the Baltimore City Police Department (BCPD) Also in 1976, the International Association of Chiefs of Police (IACP) published training guidelines which directed police to consider marital assault a crime of assault. Generally, however, the IACP training keys directed police officers to admonish or arrest the assailant and to inform and assist the victim. (Battered Women Handbook, p. 12) By early 1978, the BCPD was devoting 16 hours of intensive training to teach police officers how to deal with couples in conflict situations. The approach focused on mediating the situation, considering "arrest the least acceptable option." One LAB staff attorney emphasized that "police should be more concerned about the victim's immediate safety than merely resolving a dispute." (Pawlyna, 1978)

In early 1977, the Governor's Commission to Study the Implementation of the Equal Rights Amendment drafted two bills, both sponsored by Delegate Pauline Menes. House

Bill 124 would permit a married person to sue a spouse
for damages resulting from assault and battery, and House
Bill 32 would require the Maryland State Police to keep
records on spousal assault. Enid Sefcovic, a staff reporter
with *The News American* who had written a number of
articles on battered women, commented in a column about
the bills, "Numerous reports and articles in the past two
years established that banging one's wife around happens
more often than most Americans would like to think–and
with no legal recourse for the injured mate under current
laws." (Stefcovic, 1977) The bill requiring the Maryland
State Police to furnish the legislature with statistics on the
incidence of battered women statewide passed. By 1979,
the state police published "Maryland Battered Spouse
Report" for the period December 1, 1977, to November 30,
1978, furnishing the legislature with statistics, as required by
law. The report revealed that statewide there were 15,312
assaults between spouses reported to the police, of which
7,335 were in Baltimore City and 4,292 in Baltimore County.
Females were predominately the victims. (House of Ruth
Newsletter, May 1979)

   Friedman began working on drafting legislation to
acquire funding for shelters. The proposed legislation,
if enacted, would mandate the Department of Human
Resources to fund more than one shelter throughout the
state. One of three sponsoring senators, Senator Rosalie
Silber Abrams, from Baltimore City, introduced the bill as
Senate Bill 776. In the House of Delegates the same bill was

introduced as House Joint Resolution 32. The LAB, NOW,
the Governor's Commission to Study the Implementation of
the Equal Rights Amendment, the MCW and other women's
organizations lobbied for the passage of this legislation. As it
worked its way through the legislative session, amendments
resulted in funding mandated for only one model shelter. In
April 1977, the legislation passed directing the Department
of Human Resources to establish a model crisis shelter in
the state. It did not include an appropriation, which caused
a delay in the funding of a program to a year later because
the department's budget did not anticipate the expenditure
for the fiscal year 1976–1977. Once the House of Ruth was
organized, it submitted a proposal, written by Schuyler, to
the Department of Human Resources, for the funding of the
House of Ruth as the model crisis shelter. Senator Abrams
supported the grant application.

XI. Stability and Momentum

Beginning in January 1978, the Baltimore Chapter of the Grand Knights spent many Saturdays renovating the basement for use as a play area for the children. (Schuyler Letter to Editor, *The Sun*, January 16, 1978) By February 1978, 44 women, both black and white and ranging from ages 25 to 35, and 42 children had sheltered at the program. Most were from Baltimore City. (Baltimore Report on Battered Women) At the end of the year, there were 217 women and 250 children who had received services from a staff that had increased to five full-time and three part-time employees, supplemented by 75 volunteers. (House of Ruth Newsletter, June 1979)

Then-Congresswoman Barbara Mikulski visited the shelter to share dinner with residents and attend a Battered Women Together meeting. She discussed legislation she introduced in the House of Representatives regarding battered women and sought input from the residents. The Mikulski-sponsored Domestic Violence Prevention and Treatment Act of 1977 was the first legislative effort on the federal level.

Women were often reluctant to attend support
groups that had the word "battered women" in
the titles. We learned that if we called the group
"Women who love too much" (a popular book in
the 1970s) they were comfortable attending.
– Barbara J. Parker

The Baltimore City Police Department sent representatives to the shelter frequently to discuss security measures.
Representatives from other agencies such as the North
Baltimore Center, Union Memorial Hospital, and the
States Attorney's Office attended meetings at the shelter to
acquaint themselves with the program. (Baltimore Report
on Battered Women)

Hope for the long-term prospects of the House of
Ruth increased as a result of the Department of Human
Resources naming the program Maryland's model
domestic violence center, which brought state funding
in August 1978. The state granted the available $50,000
to the city-based program because Secretary Richard
A. Batterton said Baltimore had "the highest number of
reported wife-beatings in Maryland ... 337 of 744 cases
during January, 1978. ..." (Shelter for women gets grant,
The Sun) In addition, the Mayor's Office of Manpower
Resources funded three staff positions with money from
the Comprehensive Employment Training Administration
(CETA) under a 1973 Federal Act. (The Baltimore Report
on Battered Women) One of these employees was a former

battered wife. (Price, 1978) The CETA employees enabled
the shelter to provide a range of services which included
counseling for residents to improve self-esteem and decision
making skills; child care provided through the Displaced
Homemakers Center; and telephone reception service.
Donations flowed in from private organizations, such as the
Federation of Jewish Women and Links, an organization and
association of black women.

New Building

The condition of the original house where the shelter
was located remained a concern. It was more dilapidated
and bug infested than the board had realized at first. Due
to limited space the shelter had to turn away more women
and children than it could accommodate. Councilwoman
Mary Pat Clarke came to the rescue. Through her efforts
and Mayor William Donald Schaefer's support, the City
of Baltimore Department of Housing and Community
Development (HCD) committed $50,000 of federal
Community Block Grant funds to refurbish a city-owned
house, including a redesigned floor plan. HCD rented it to
the House of Ruth for $1 per year. Clarke, overcoming some
concerns, garnered support from the Barclay-Greenmount
neighborhood association. At the May annual meeting of
the House of Ruth Clarke commented, "The House of Ruth
has taken a concept and made it understandable and so real
that in a brief period of time it has created a cause that can
help people." (Dickman, 1978) Toward the end of 1978, the

move a few doors north to 2417 North Calvert Street went
smoothly.

Statewide Interest

In January 1979, the MCW, the House of Ruth,
Montgomery County Abused Persons' Program and Court
Appointed Special Advocates (CASA) Howard County
formed a statewide coalition named the Maryland Network
Against Domestic Violence (MNADV) It began with a
loose-knit group of concerned service providers who met
regularly under the auspice of the MCW. The planning stage
had begun the previous year. The MNADV's goal was to
enable the domestic violence movement to expand into
other areas vital to its growth by bringing together service
providers, allied professionals and concerned citizens to
enhance the common effort to reduce family violence. The
next decade saw immense growth in the House of Ruth
program and others around the state.

The Mayor's Office brought together criminal justice
representatives with advocates for battered spouses to write
a grant application, which was submitted to the federal Law
Enforcement Assistance Administration (LEAA) to address
family violence. The House of Ruth anticipated receiving
some of the funds, but unfortunately, the grant was not
approved. The effort, nevertheless, heightened awareness of
those involved and increased momentum. In February 1980,
the Governor's Commission on Law Enforcement and the
Administration of Justice awarded LEAA grants in the total

amount of $51,000 to provide funding to support counseling for children, a legal advocacy program, and to expand the existing therapy effort for batterers.

The grant allowed Andre Papantonio to join Fran Fitch as a co-therapist. Fitch was a clinical associate professor of psychiatry at University of Maryland and formerly a therapist at the University Hospital. (Fear, pain, humiliation explode in wife-beating: Therapy group helps batterers understand their suppressed feeling, *The Sun*)

More legislation brought important protections to abused women. In 1979, the General Assembly passed gender-neutral legislation requiring police to accompany an abused spouse to her or his home to obtain personal belongings. The Protection from Domestic Violence Act prepared by the Annapolis Women's Law Center in 1978 failed that year, but when introduced again in 1979 by the Senate Judicial Proceedings Committee and the Majority Leader, Rosalie Abrams (SB 159), it became established law. Also, the previous year, the Court of Appeals of Maryland in the case of *Lusby v. Lusby* abolished inter-spousal tort immunity for intentional outrageous injury.

The efforts to glean community support continued to reap rewards. A benefit auction at the Maryland Historical Society in the spring attracted more than 250 persons who listened to jazz by the Fuzzy Kane Trio and Ruby Glover, a noted jazz singer, who worked with the Battered Wives Task Force. Maryland first lady Pat Hughes donated a "personally guided tour of the Governor's Mansion" for

10 people. (Rubenstein, 1979) Other auction items included lunch with Mayor Schaefer, a hat from actor Alan Alda and a baseball autographed by Orioles third baseman Brooks Robinson. (Bennett, 1979)

A disco skate-a-thon, "Roll in the Money," was held in November at Skateland, Painters Mill Road. Over 200 people attended. (House of Ruth Newsletter, December, 1979) The shelter received contributions from proceeds of luncheons, teas and boutique sales held by the Dulaney Valley Women's Club, Inc., the American Association of University Women and the National Council of Jewish Women, respectively. Parker remembers the Baltimore City Fair that year she volunteered at the House of Ruth booth where numerous visitors stopped by with a donation saying "you helped my mother (or friend or sister)." Throughout the year numerous individuals, organizations and businesses made contributions, among them the Morris Goldseker Foundation, Henry and Ruth Blaustein Rosenberg Foundation, Sigma Phi Gamma International Sorority, Polock Johnny's, McCormack and Company , Gunpowder Jaycee Women's Organization, Fox Chevrolet, Women's Club of Catonsville, and United Methodist Women of Timonium. (House of Ruth Newsletters, October, 1979 and December, 1979)

At year's end, private support amounted to $65,107 and fees and grants from government agencies reached $164,037. Revenues exceeded expenses, allowing the House of Ruth to develop a healthy reserve to support continued growth.

(Annual Fiscal Report – Charitable Organization, The
House of Ruth, Baltimore, Inc.)

In spite of the funding challenges, as early as February
1978, President Marcella Schuyler remained optimistic. She
envisioned a bright future. By the fall of 1978, the Baltimore
Task Force on Battered Women merged with the House of
Ruth. In Issue 1 of "Baltimore Report on Battered Women,"
the joint publication of the two groups, she commented to
readers, "The future of the House of Ruth looks bright, 'with
a little help from our friends.' And so, with a little help from
you and others, the House of Ruth will continue to respond
to the desperate need of many women."

With the help of countless volunteers and supporters
over the past 35 years, hope for its future continues to shine
brightly.

AFTERWORD

In its 35-year history, the House of Ruth has had only five executive directors, a credit to its stability and to one person in particular, Carole Alexander. After Benshoff left to return to Pennsylvania in late 1978, Mary Louise Mussoline became executive director and stayed two and a half years. In 1981, Bettye Williams replaced Mussoline. Then, in 1983, Carole Alexander began a tenure that lasted 27 years, which included, among many accomplishments, the move to the House of Ruth's present Montebello site, increased services, and a budget in the millions of dollars.

During the first 10 years, when the challenges were the hardest, the following individuals served as president and solidified the founding of the House of Ruth in Baltimore:

1977–1978	Marcella Schuyler
1979	Karen Kelley
1980–81	Joyce Kroeller
1981–82	Kathleen Ellis
1982–84	Marilyn Maultsby
1985	Carole Maier
1986–87	Jodi Dunn

Epilogue by Sandi Timmons, Executive Director, House of Ruth Maryland

From the bold, tenacious work of the people you've read about in *That It May Be Well With You,* the House of Ruth Maryland has evolved and grown. Our emergency shelter is now a building with 23 rooms plus 6 extended-stay apartments that houses 84 women and children at any given time, and has a nurse-run clinic on site. We have added a rapid re-housing program to relocate women in the community and quickly create stability for them and their children. Legal help for victims now comes from a full legal clinic within the agency, with staff attorneys working in courthouses throughout the city and surrounding counties to help clients secure protection orders, and some divorce and custody cases. In order to address the complexity of the control an abuser exerts, we provide several forms of clinical services, both individually and in group settings. We work with every police district in Baltimore City to reach out to the victims of all intimate partner violence (IPV) related calls officers go out on, in order to offer services and support. With the exception of a few highly committed volunteers, our 24/7 Hotline is staffed by employees who are specifically skilled at handling crisis calls and are knowledgeable regarding the community support services that are also available to callers.

Our Founding Mothers were the embodiment of a passion for changing attitudes, behaviors and systems that perpetuate intimate partner violence. We're proud to continue to move that work forward, with equal passion. We have a strong, highly respected presence in Annapolis and both introduce and support legislation that is beneficial to victims of IPV. We provide training to judges, sheriffs, police departments, social workers, employees of social services agencies, medical professionals and employers to educate the community about the dynamics of intimate partner violence, how to recognize it, and how to respond. To break the cycle of abuse, we work with both abusers and the children of the violent household. Our Gateway program takes abusers, who are largely court ordered, through a process of getting him to acknowledge his behavior, agree that it's wrong, and identify how to change that behavior. The results of recent studies about the effects on children are informing our work with them, both to keep them from becoming the next generation of abusers and victims, and to help heal the damage. We now have a program for children who witness a parental homicide. Ideally, it is prevention that ends IPV, and that work takes us to schools to talk to young people about healthy relationships.

As we look to the future, we believe strongly in the need to radically shift thinking. The House of Ruth Maryland will draw the community to conversation around the source of the issue — the behavior of the abuser. We have begun to engage men in the movement, to speak out and to model values and belief systems that refuse to tolerate any attitude that power over, and control of, a partner is acceptable. We continue to build momentum toward achieving our vision that "One day, every woman in Maryland will be safe in her own home."

APPENDIX A

Baltimore Task Force on Battered Women

- Eva Barczak, Past State Regent, Catholic Daughters of America
- Olga Brunning, Attorney, Public Defenders Office
- Lynn Deutschman, Former Public School Teacher and Civic Activist
- Marian Finney, Volunteer
- Brian Gamble, Social Worker
- Ruby Glover, Jazz Singer, Volunteer
- Marion Graham, Social Worker, Carruthers Center
- Arlene Lazarus, Women in Self Help (WISH)
- Natalie L. (Toby) Mendeloff, WISH
- Cynthia Marano, Displaced Homemakers
- Barbara J. Parker, University of Maryland School of Nursing
- Courtney Petersen, Volunteer
- Marian Perlman, WISH
- Major Roberts, Salvation Army
- Carolyn Rodis, Attorney, Legal Aid Bureau

- Marcella Schuyler, Social Worker, Baltimore NOW President
- Joanne Steger, Volunteer
- Hazel Warnick, Attorney, Legal Aid Bureau

Appendix B

Founding Members Ad Hoc Committee/First Board*

- Eva Barczak, Past State Regent of Maryland Catholic Daughters of America*
- Joy Berman, Volunteer*
- Grace Birger, Volunteer*
- Elizabeth Stanford Butterfield, Chemical Analyst, Food and Drug Administration, Federal Women's Group Volunteer*
- Shirley H. Clifford, Volunteer*
- Carol Clarinen Del Uomo, Volunteer*
- Sarah Esterhay, Volunteer*
- Kathleen O'Ferrall Friedman, Attorney, Legal Aid Bureau, Inc.
- Marion Graham, Psychiatric Social Worker, Carruthers Center
- Audrey Harris, President, Maryland Women Together*
- Lois Mulder Hemstra, Psychiatric Social Worker, Carruthers Center
- Arlene Lazarus, Women in Self-Help (WISH)*
- Kathleen McDonald, Maryland Commission for Women

- Cynthia Marano, Displaced Homemakers*
- Natalie L. (Toby) Mendeloff, Women in Self Help (WISH)*
- Ellen Moyer, Executive Director, Maryland Commission for Women*
- Marian Perlman, WISH
- Courtney Petersen, Volunteer, Chair of Foundations Committee*
- Anne Piet, Volunteer*
- Kathleen M. (Katie) Ryan, President, Maryland Women Together*
- Geraldine Salmond, Volunteer*
- Jeannene M. Sears, Women's Resource Center*
- Hazel Warnick, Attorney, Legal Aid Bureau, Women's Law Center
- Jacqueline Wayland, Volunteer*
- Barbara Ziegler, Volunteer*

*Directors who acted until the First Annual Meeting plus Marcella Schuyler and Esther Lazarus, former director of Baltimore City Department of Social Services.

ACKNOWLEDGEMENTS

This history could not have been written without the recollections of some key people. We are indebted to Lynn Deutschman, Judy Katz, Natalie L. (Toby) Mendeloff, Carolyn Rodis, Hazel Warnick and most of all to Marcella Schuyler. Thank you also to Marian Decker, Fran Fitch, Richard W. Friedman, Michael Fox and Stan Wenacur for small touches that added a great deal. We appreciate the assistance of The Greater Homewood Community Association who gave us access to their records, the Enoch Pratt Library, the Maryland Historical Society and Aiden Faust at the University of Baltimore. Documents from the Health and Welfare Council and the papers of Esther Lazarus were helpful. Susan Breaux McShea's editing helped clarify certain portions of the writing and reshape the history into a more coherent whole. We owe a debt of gratitude to Christine Langr, who was put on this earth to aid technologically challenged people. A wiz at illustration and information graphics, she enhanced old newspaper photos that would otherwise not be publishable and found many old photos on eBay. Cymone Gosnell, the Loyola student who accepted this assignment as her project was always helpful and creative. Dr. Kevin Atticks the publisher at Apprentice House is an amazing human being. He was always patient and worked with Cymone to develop the entire manuscript, including the cover. Sandi Timmins' enthusiastic support and cheerleading encouraged us throughout our research and writing.

END NOTES

Ashby, John, in collaboration with Erin Pizzey, chairman and founder of Women's Aid. "*The Problem of Battered Women,*" Chiswick, London, 1974. House of Ruth Maryland collection, Friedman papers.

Baltimore Report on Battered Women, The joint publication of the House of Ruth, Baltimore, Inc. and the Baltimore Task Force on Battered Women. Issue 1, February, 1978, pages 1-4. Health and Welfare Counsel of Central Maryland Archives, University of Baltimore.

Battered Women: A Handbook. Baltimore Task Force on Battered Women Revised Edition: April 1978. House of Ruth Maryland collection, Friedman papers.

Bennett, Allegra. "Alan Alda's hat, going, going gone." *The Sun* (1837-1987); Apr 30, 1979, ProQuest Historical Newspapers: Baltimore Sun, The (1837-1987) pg. C2.

Brager, George & Sprecht, Harry *Community Organizing.* New York and London: Columbia University Press, 1969.

"Brutality against wives linked to macho ethic". *The Sun* (1837-1987); Feb 22, 1977, ProQuest Historical Newspapers: Baltimore Sun, The (1837-1987) pg. C2.

"Club plans Christmas Party." *The Sun* (1837-1987); Dec 11, 1977, ProQuest

Historical Newspapers: Baltimore Sun, The (1837-1987) pg. E25.

Deutschman, Lynn, House of Ruth Founding Project, Questionnaire, August 2013. Deutschman reported, "Years later, my home was on House and Garden Television and I received a phone call from my husband's secretary, now living in Florida. ... she was on her own and making a wonderful life for herself and her son. She called because she had seen the show and wanted to make contact to thank us for helping her turn her life around. A perfect circle to the entire program and to my personal involvement as well."

Dickman, Sharon., "Some Women Put Up With Abuse." *The Evening Sun,* Monday, March 29, 1976. House of Ruth Maryland collection, Friedman papers.

Dickman, Sharon" New Home Due For Battered." *The Evening Sun*, May 21, 1978. House of Ruth Maryland collection.

"Dinner theatre trip set." *The Sun* (1837-1987); Mar 26, 1978, ProQuest Historical Newspapers: Baltimore Sun, The (1837-1987) pg.E15.

Donaldson, Susan K. "Breakthroughs in Scientific Research: The Discipline of Nursing, 1960-1999", *Annual Review of Nursing Research_* 18 (1), 247-311. 2000.

Durban, Karin, "Wife beating", *Ladies Home Journal.* June 1974.

Eisenberg, Sue E. and Micklow, Patricia L. "The Assaulted Wife: Catch 22' Revisited", *Women's Rights Law Reporter*, Vol.3: 1977, pp.138-161.

"Esther Lazarus, welfare chief in city till 1968, dies at 80." *The Sun* (1837-1987); June 18, 1980, ProQuest Historical Newspapers: Baltimore Sun, The (1837-1987) pg.B1.

Federal Bureau of Investigation (FBI), *Uniform Crime Reports for the United States*, Washington, D.C.: U.S. Government Printing Office, 1967.

Federal Bureau of Investigation (FBI), *Uniform Crime Reports for the United States,* Washington, D.C.: U.S. Government Printing Office, 1973.

Fojtik, Kathleen M. *Wife Beating: How to Develop a Wife Assault Task Force and Project,* An Arbor, Michigan, Domestic Violence and Spousal Assault Fund, Now, Inc., 1976. House of Ruth Maryland collection, Friedman papers. This "how-to" manual includes "Overview of Washtenaw County Police Data: 1974 Cases of Wife Assault. The report contains the following statistics:

In Washtenaw County, 43% of the total number of assault and battery cases involved assault against wives.

Twenty-seven percent of felonious assaults were against wives.

In murder cases, 33% of the victims were wives.

In Ypsilanti County, 40% of assault and battery cases were against wives; 23% of felonious assault, and 20% of intent to murder.

"Food drive set up for House of Ruth." *The Sun* (1837-1987); April 28, 1978, ProQuest Historical Newspapers: Baltimore Sun, The (1837-1987) pg.C6.

Friedan, Betty. *The Feminine Mystique.* New York: W.W. Norton, 1963

Friedman, Kathleen O'Ferrall. *Battered Women: A Manual For Survival.* Baltimore. Women's Law Center. 1976. House of Ruth Maryland collection, Friedman Papers. Friedman revised the pamphlet, which was published in a professional format as *Survival Manual, Battered Women* in 1977 by the Maryland Commission for Women.

Friedman, Kathleen O'Ferrall, "When Did You Stop Beating Your Wife?" The *University of Maryland Law Forum,* Volume VI, No.2, 1976, pp. 39-47.

Friedman. Kathleen O'Ferrall, "The Image of Battered Women", *American Journal of Public Health*, Vol.67, No.8, August 1977, pp. 722-723.

Friedman, Kathleen O'Ferrall., Peterson, Roger., Parker, Barbara., *Inter-spousal Assault in Maryland: A Survey Report on Women.* Maryland Department of Human Resources (DHR Pub 5007), 1979.

Friedman, Kathleen O'Ferrall, *It's About NOW* (Anne Arundel County NOW), Vol.6, No.1, February, 1978. House of Ruth Maryland collection, Friedman papers.

Friedman, Kathleen O'Ferrall and Schuyler, Marcella., *Timeline/Wife Abuse: Chronology of the Battered Women's Movement for the State of Maryland.* House of Ruth Maryland collection, Friedman papers.

Gelles, Richard J., "Abused Wives: Why Do They Stay?" *Journal of Marriage and the Family*, November, 1976, pp. 659-668.

Gelles, Richard J., *The Violent Home: A Study of Physical Aggression between Husbands and Wives.* Beverly Hills: Sage Publications, 1972.

Gingold, Judith., "One of These Days –Pow! Right in the Kisser: The Truth about Battered Wives," *Ms.* Vol. V, No.2, August 1976.

Greater Homewood Community Corporation By-Laws, Section 1.01. General Purposes, approved April 28, 1970. Greater Homewood Community Corporation collection.

Greater Homewood Community Corporation Minutes, October 27, 1970 to January 19, 1972. Greater Homewood Community Corporation collection.

Hayden, Casey & King, Mary., *Sex and Caste – A Kind of Memo*, "Liberation," April 1966. iuc.edu/orgs/cwluherstory/CWLUArchive/

memo.html. King and Hayden, members of the Student Nonviolent
Coordinating Committee (SNCC), wrote this position paper objecting
to women's subordinate role in the civil rights movement.

"Help for battered women available" *The Sun* (1937-1987); Dec 22, 1976;
ProQuest Historical Newspapers: Baltimore Sun, The (1837-1987) pg.
B8.

Henderson, Randi., "Shelters aren't solution but they help", The Sun(1837-
1987): Mar 23, 1977; ProQuest Historical Newspapers: Baltimore Sun,
The (1837-1987) pg.B1.

House of Ruth newsletter, May 1979, House of Ruth of Maryland
collection.

James, Ellen L. "Homey Place In Charles Village: Refuge Near For
battered Women," *Baltimore: The Evening Sun*, Wednesday, October
12, 1977. House of Ruth Maryland collection, Friedman papers.

Katz, Judith B., House of Ruth Founding Project, Questionnaire, May,
2013.

Legal Aid Bureau, Inc., "National Organization of (sic) Women, Women's
Law Center, Inc. Symposium on Battered Women", Baltimore,
Maryland Saturday, April 3, 1976: Agenda and Evaluation, House of
Ruth Maryland, Schuyler Papers.

Let Her Voice Be Heard, Pamphlet published by House of Ruth in
celebration of the first decade, 1988, House of Ruth Maryland
collection, Friedman Papers.

Lewis, Jone Johnson, "Presidents Commission on the Status of Women,
1961-1963", womenshistory.about.com/od/laws/a/status_women.htm.

Lusby v. Lusby, 283 Md. 334, 390 A. 2d 77 (1978)

Martin, Del. *Battered Wives*. San Francisco: Glide Publication, 1976.

Martin, Del, "Battered Women," *The New York Times*, October 1975.

Mendeloff, Natalie M. (Toby), House of Ruth Founding Project, Interview, June 24, 2013.

"Ms. Steinem To Host 'Tragedy of Battered Wives,'" Baltimore: *The Evening Sun*, Monday, April 11, 1977. House of Ruth Maryland collection, Friedman papers.

Napikoski, Linda, "Equal Rights Amendment: Constitutional Equality and Justice for All?" womenshistory.about.com/od/equalrightsamendment/a/equal_rights_amendment_overview.htm, no date.

O'Brien, John E., "Violence in Divorce Prone Families." *Journal Of Marriage And The Family* (November 1971)

Parker, Barbara. & Schumacher, Dale. "The Battered Wife Syndrome and Violence in the Nuclear Family of Origin: A Controlled Pilot Study," *American Journal of Public Health*, Vol. 67, No. 8 August 1977, pp. 760 -761.

Pawlyna, Andrea. "A Refuge for Beaten Women," *Baltimore: The Sunday Sun*, Baltimore, Sunday, January 1, 1978. House of Ruth Maryland collection, Friedman papers.

Peterson, Bill, "System Frustrates Battered Wives," Washington, D.C.: *The Washington Post*, Sunday, November, 2, 1975. House of Ruth Maryland collection, Friedman papers.

Peterson, Bill, "Battered Wife Syndrome: Shame, Fear Keep Most Women Silent," Washington, D.C.: *The Washington Post*, Saturday, September 13, 1975. House of Ruth Maryland collection, Friedman papers.

Pizzey, Erin. *Scream Quietly or the Neighbors Will Hear.* London: Coventure and Penguin Press, 1974. Short Hills, NJ: Ridley Enslow Publishers (American Edition), 1977.

Plummer, Sara."History of domestic violence policy" salomemagazine. com/chamber.php?id=178, 2006.

Price, Joyce, "Refuge For Battered Women May Close Without Funding", Baltimore: *The News American*, Sunday, February 26, 1978. House of Ruth Maryland collection, Friedman papers.

Program on battered women, The Sun (1937-1987); Mar 6, 1977; *ProQuest Historical Newspapers: Baltimore Sun, The* (1837-1987) pg. D6.

Renhert, Isaac, "For you troubled, battered women, the number is 433-9400", *The Sun* (1837-1987); June 1, 1978, ProQuest Historical Newspapers: *The Baltimore Sun*, (1837-1987) pg. B1.

Rodis, Carolyn, House of Ruth Founding Project, Questionnaire, August 2013. In her answers to the questionnaire Rodis refers to The Honorable Robert B. Watts, who served on the Circuit Court for Baltimore City from 1968-1985.

Rubenstein, Terry., "Harry would rather be Governor than pitch for the Yanks; Pat never doubted it", *The Sun* (1837-1987); May 29, 1979, ProQuest Historical Newspapers: Baltimore Sun, The (1837-1987) pg. B1.

Schuyler, Marcella. *An Analysis of the Battered Wives Problem*, submitted to University of Maryland School of Social Work, December 8, 1975, House of Ruth Maryland collection, Friedman and Schuyler papers.

Schuyler, Marcella, "Battered Wives: An Emerging Social Problem," *Social Work*, Vol. 21, No.6, November 1976.

Schuyler, Marcella, House of Ruth Founding Project, Interview, March 11, 2013.

Schuyler, Marcella, House of Ruth Founding Project, Questionnaire, March 3, 2013.

Schuyler, Marcella. Untitled and undated comments to a public gathering, 1978, House of Ruth Maryland collection, Schuyler papers.

Schuyler, Marcella, "President, House of Ruth Baltimore, MD: Testimony on Legislative Proposals Concerning Inter-spousal Abuse". Undated. House of Ruth Maryland collection, Schuyler Papers

Sefcovic, Enid. "Battered Wives: A Shelter From The Pain", Baltimore: *The News American*, Wednesday, June 18, 1975. House of Ruth Maryland collection, Friedman papers.

Sefcovic, Enid., Baltimore: *The News American*, 1977. House of Ruth Maryland collection, Friedman papers.

"Social concern conference focuses on battered women," Baltimore: *The Sun*, Tuesday, November 30, 1976. House of Ruth Maryland collection, Friedman papers.

Sterling, Joy, "Refuge For Battered Wives", Baltimore: *The Daily Record*, Wednesday, November 3, 1976. House of Ruth Maryland collection, Friedman papers.

Steinmetz, Susan and Straus, Murray A. *Violence in the Family*.

New York: Harper and Row, 1974.

Straus, Murray A., Gelles, Richard J., and Steinmetz, Suzanne K. "Violence in the Family: An Assessment of Knowledge and Research Needs." Paper presented to the American Association for the Advancement of Science, Boston, February 23, 1976.

Waite, Linda J. "U.S. Women at Work," Population Bulletin, Vol.36, No.2, Washington, D.C.: Population Reference Bureau, Inc., May 1981, <u>rand. org/pubs/reports/2008/R2824.pdf</u>.

Warnick, Hazel, House of Ruth Founding Project, Questionnaire, April, 2013.

Warrior, Betsy, *Wifebeating*. Somerville: New England Free Press 1975a .

Warrior, Betsy, *Battered Lives*. Pittsburg: KNOW Inc. 1975b

"Wife-Abuse Symposium Scheduled," Baltimore: *The Evening Sun*, Wednesday, March 24, 1976. House of Ruth Maryland collection, Friedman papers.

"Women's Fair slated", *The Sun* (1837-1987); Feb 10, 1976, ProQuest Historical Newspapers: *The Baltimore Sun*, (1837-1987) pg. B 10.

Worobec, Mary, "Progress Slow In Treatment of Battered Wives", Baltimore: *The News American*, Wednesday, March 30, 1977. House of Ruth Maryland Collection, Friedman papers.

THE AUTHORS

Kathleen O'Ferrall Friedman, a retired judge of the
Circuit Court for Baltimore City, grew up in Baltimore.
After graduating from College of Notre Dame of Maryland

and the University of
Maryland School of Law,
she received her MSW
from the University of
Pennsylvania School
of Social Work. While
pursuing her education,
she worked as a junior
high school teacher,
juvenile probation officer,
and in social work field
placements. A lawyer at
the Legal Aid Bureau in

*The authors (left, Friedman and right, Parker)
posed after interviewing Marcella Schuyler
(center), first president of the House of Ruth,
Sarasota Florida in May 2013.*

the 1970s, Friedman encountered numerous divorce clients
who confided incidents of battering by intimate partners.
While not practicing social work at the Bureau, it was her
understanding of social policy and practice that inspired her

to use both the law and social work disciplines for social change on behalf of abused women.

Dr. Barbara J. Parker has been actively researching violence against women since 1975. With numerous colleagues, her program of research was the first to document the incidence of violence in the year before pregnancy (19%) and during pregnancy (15%) These statistical findings have subsequently been replicated and validated in countless other studies. In another study, she tested an empowerment intervention for abused women that significantly reduced the amount of violence the research participants were experiencing one year later. This intervention has been publicized by the March of Dimes and is used extensively in the U.S. and internationally. Her more recent work described the experiences of children who grew up in a home where one parent killed the other. She was the Theresa A. Thomas Professor of Nursing at the University of Virginia School of Nursing from 1993 until her retirement in 2012. She is a fellow in the American Academy of Nursing, past president of the Nursing Network on Violence Against Women International, and was named Distinguished Nurse Researcher in 2000 by the Southern Nursing Research Society. In 2004, she received an award for excellence in research from the Nursing Network on Violence Against Women International She has published extensively on violence against women, nursing scholarship and homicide.

Apprentice House is the country's only campus-based, student-staffed book publishing company. Directed by professors and industry professionals, it is a nonprofit activity of the Communication Department at Loyola University Maryland.

Using state-of-the-art technology and an experiential learning model of education, Apprentice House publishes books in untraditional ways. This dual responsibility as publishers and educators creates an unprecedented collaborative environment among faculty and students, while teaching tomorrow's editors, designers, and marketers.

Outside of class, progress on book projects is carried forth by the AH Book Publishing Club, a co-curricular campus organization supported by Loyola University Maryland's Office of Student Activities.

Eclectic and provocative, Apprentice House titles intend to entertain as well as spark dialogue on a variety of topics. Financial contributions to sustain the press's work are welcomed. Contributions are tax deductible to the fullest extent allowed by the IRS.

To learn more about Apprentice House books or to obtain submission guidelines, please visit www.apprenticehouse.com.

Apprentice House
Communication Department
Loyola University Maryland
4501 N. Charles Street
Baltimore, MD 21210
Ph: 410-617-5265 • Fax: 410-617-2198
info@apprenticehouse.com • www.apprenticehouse.com

CPSIA information can be obtained at www.ICGtesting.com
Printed in the USA
BVOW04s0338230414

351464BV00010B/336/P